FESTIVALS

Harvest festival
Sukkot
Hallowe'en
Diwali
Chanukah
Christmas
Chinese New Year

Holi
Pesach
Easter in Cyprus
Easter
Eid ul Fitr
Carnival

Oxford University Press Music Department, Walton Street, Oxford OX2 6DP

Festivals (covering Harvest, Sukkot, Hallowe'en, Diwali, Chanukah, Christmas, Chinese New Year, Holi, Pesach, Easter in Cyprus, Easter, Eid-ul-Fitr, Carnival)

First published 1986
Reprinted 1988, 1990, and 1991
Resources updated 1990
ISBN 0 19 3212854

Designed by Ann Samuel
Illustrated by Jan Nesbitt
Printed in Hong Kong

Acknowledgments

I am indebted to many people who have helped me during the time I have been compiling material for these festival topics.

Chanukah, Sukkot and Pesach
The Rev. Reuben Turner, Director of Youth and Education, Jewish National Fund for Great Britain and Ireland, assisted me initially in preparing these sections, making available song material, suitable literature and reading a first script. Mrs Rita Kalev, Headteacher, Simon Marks Jewish Primary School, and Mrs Eve Benjamin, Hebrew teacher, Matilda Marks Kennedy School, both of London, suggested songs and provided translations from the Hebrew. I would like to thank Ms Shifra Manor, music teacher at Simon Marks Jewish Primary School, for her version of the folk songs and for her advice on the setting of the songs in these sections.

Diwali and Holi
Punitha Perinparaja, teacher in Brent, researched Indian music, song and dance at the Institute of Education. She has given invaluable help and support in the preparation of these sections, offering her own song compositions and activities tried out by her in her area and assisting with the translations. Mrs Subbash Mukker, teacher at Duncombe Infants School, London, obtained material from her home in India and recorded her own song for inclusion here.

Chinese New Year
I gathered material from many sources. I would like to thank: Mr Barton, Headmaster, St James and St Peter's Primary School, London. Mrs Gaik See Choo, music teacher at the above school, who read a first script, gave me comments and suggestions and contributed the 'Boat song' which she uses in her own teaching. Miss Louise C. Cheng, Lecturer, Institute of Education, Singapore, who sent me material from her own collection.

Easter in Cyprus
This section would not have materialized without the enthusiastic involvement of Mrs Nitsa Sergides, teacher, Pakeman Primary School, London, and Mrs Maria Roussou, Greek coordinator of the Schools Council Mother Tongue Project. I am most grateful for all their help and contributions. I would like to thank Mr Miltiades Erotokritou, music teacher working with the Greek Parents' Association for his help in the selection of songs and for translating from the Greek.

Eid-ul-Fitr
I am grateful to Mr and Mrs Chowdhury for the music and words to the Prayer to the Prophet Muhammad. Mrs Hiron Alam, musician and teacher, introduced me to the song by Kazi Nazrul, composed two songs for this section, assisted with the translation of these and other songs and contributed the recipe 'Dimer pita'. I thank her for her help and for the delightful working afternoons we spent together.

Carnival
Mr Len Garrison of the Afro-Caribbean Education Resource Project kindly allowed me the use of books and resources at his centre and Barbara Romain, teacher on exchange from Trinidad, loaned me some of her own music books from Trinidad. The final script of this section owes much to the careful reading of Mr Ansell Wong and to detail supplied by Miss Audrey Dennett, former Inspector for Music, ILEA.

My thanks are due to the following for help and advice which was sought and most generously given:
Miss Margaret Clucas, Headteacher, Alexandra Infants School, London
Mrs Elizabeth Singleton, teacher, Alexandra Infants School, London
Mrs Anne Waters, Headteacher, Earlham Infants School, London
Mr J Wight, Inspector for Multi-Ethnic Education, ILEA
Dr Helen Kanitker, School for Oriental Studies, London
Mrs Julia Griffiths, my colleague, who undertook the job of reading right through, with many valuable comments.
Mrs Leonora Davies, Music Coordinator, ILEA, who read the music manuscript.
Miss Dorothy Taylor, Adviser, Religious Education, ILEA, for the many discussions we had on the religious content of this book.
Philippa Whitbread who commissioned and shaped the manuscript.

Acknowledgements

Harvest Festival
Songs
Wendy van Blankenstein ('I can see cherries')
Boosey & Hawkes Ltd ('Picking up conkers' ('Finding') from *Let's join in* © copyright 1963 by Boosey & Hawkes Music Publishers Ltd)
Harmony Music Ltd ('This world goes round and round')
Jane Morgan ('Harvest in the city')
National Christian Education Council ('Fishermen' from *New Child Songs*)
Society of Brothers Ltd ('Autumn is here')
Stainer and Bell Ltd ('World Harvest')
Akon Udonwa ('Look at us and watch us')
Poems
Bell & Hyman Ltd ('Bread' by H. E. Wilkinson and 'Red in Autumn' by Elizabeth Gould from *The Book of 1000 Poems*)
Dobson Books Ltd ('Harvest Home' by Leonard Clark from *Collected Poems and Verses for Children*)
Doubleday & Co. Inc. ('Vegetables' by Rachel Field from *Taxis and Toadstools* © 1926 Doubleday & Co. Inc., first published in Great Britain 1962)
Vernon Scannell ('From Autumn' from *A Flock of Words* (1969))

Sukkot
Jewish National Fund ('Happy Festival' (Yom Tov Lanu))

Hallowe'en
Songs
Jean Gilbert ('The witch')
Harcourt Brace Jovanovich Inc. ('Hallowe'en' from *The Little Hill*)
Jane Morgan ('Witch watch')
Novello & Co. Ltd ('Hansel and Gretel')
Poems
Atheneum Publishers Inc. ('Witch goes shopping' by Lilian Moore from *See My Lovely Poison Ivy*)
Doubleday & Co. Inc. ('Witch, Witch' by Rose Fyleman from *Fifty-one New Nursery Rhymes* copyright 1931. Reprinted by permission of the Publishers)
William Heinemann Ltd ('Old Moll' by James Reeves from *The Wandering Moon*)
Jack Prelutsky ('Wild witches' ball')

Diwali
Songs
Subbash Mukker ('Diwali')
Punitha Perinparaja ('The story of Diwali in song')

Chanukah
Poem
Behrman House Publishers Inc. ('My Hanukkah candles' by Philip M. Raskin)

Christmas
Songs
Oliver & Boyd ('Baby Jesus I sing to you' from *Celebration Songs*)
Oxford University Press (words of 'Carol' by Francis B. Wood from *Sixty Songs for Little Children* and words of 'Zither Carol' by Malcolm Sargent)
Stainer and Bell Ltd ('Child for the World')
June Witham ('The gifts' from *Carol, Gaily carol* published by A & C Black Ltd)
Poems
Marchette Chute ('Christmas')
Joan Mellings ('Christmas in two lands')

Chinese New Year
Songs
Gaik See Choo ('Boat song')
Low Siew Poh ('Chinese New Year is here again')
Oxford University Press ('Lantern Song' from *Lantern Song Book*)
Poems
Penguin Books Ltd ('Quiet night thoughts' by Li Po and 'Wandering breezes' by Tu Fu from *Li Po and Tu Fu* translated by Arthur Cooper (Penguin Classics, 1973) pp.109, 205. Copyright © Arthur Cooper 1973)

Holi
Songs
Punitha Perinparaja ('Holi festival of colour')
Unicef ('Stick dance' from *Understanding Our Neighbors*)

Pesach
Song
Sterling Publishing Co. Inc. ('Dayenu' from *Holiday Singing and Dancing* by Esther Nelson)
Poem
Purnell Books ('The Seder' by Philip M. Raskin from *Festival Joy*)

Easter in Cyprus
Music Sales, 78 Newman St., London W1 ('Won't you pass, Mistress Mary' © copyright 1968 Oak Publications (a division of Music Sales Corp., New York, USA))

Easter
Songs
Blackie and Son Ltd ('Pace Egg Song')
Chappell Music Ltd ('Spring is coming' and 'The little seed' from *Ways with Music – Wonderful World* by Christina Brice and Geoffrey Winters)
Jane Morgan ('Easter trip')
National Christian Education Council ('New life in Spring' from *New Child Songs*)
Oxford University Press ('When Easter to the dark world came' words by W. H. Hamilton (1886–1958) from *Children Praising*)
Stainer and Bell Ltd ('Round for the coming of Spring' and 'When Easter to the dark world came' (music arrangement))
Poems
Bell & Hyman Ltd ('Snowdrops' by Mary Vivian and 'Welcome to Spring' by Irene Thompson from *The Book of 1000 Poems*)
Stainer and Bell Ltd ('Seed song' by Christopher Rowe)

Eid-ul-Fitr
Songs
Hiron Alam ('A beautiful day' and 'Eid moon')

Carnival
Songs
Boosey & Hawkes Ltd ('Johny Grotto' from *Folk Songs of Trinidad and Tobago* Collected and arranged by Olive Walke © copyright 1970 by Boosey & Hawkes Music Publishers Ltd)
Columbus Publishers Ltd ('Congo Tay' and 'Linky Loo' from *Let us Play* by E. Robertson)
Poems
Columbus Publishers Ltd ('Humming Bird' and 'Iguana' from *Joy of Nature in the West Indies*)

Introduction

Festivals form an integral part of the culture of any society. In Britain ones like Harvest Festival, Hallowe'en, Christmas and Easter have been traditionally included in the school curriculum through music, song, stories and relevant classroom activities.

Today our society includes people from many different cultural backgrounds and the children in our schools reflect the multi-ethnic groupings in various parts of the country. Many teachers are seeking to include the festivals that are celebrated by the children they teach and by their families so that children from different cultures will learn about one another. 'In growing to appreciate the traditions of others they may come to respect their own culture and that of their neighbour – a hope for a multicultural society' (Dr. Desmond Brennen from 'Religious Education and the multicultural society').

This anthology outlines a selection of popular festivals, each presented in the form of a musical topic, and includes:

a short introduction to the festival;
classroom activities including art and craft, music, reference to festival food and a recipe(s);
songs and singing games with teaching notes;
poems and/or a story with suggestions for dramatic work and musical accompaniment;
bibliography of teacher's and children's reference books, story books, recorded music and useful addresses grouped in the main resource section.

In the case of all the festivals from other countries one of the most valuable sources of help and information will be the children and parents from those countries, and the involvement of interested parents will add to the enjoyment of the celebration of those festivals.

The collection and research of much of this material has taken me into many different corners of the large metropolis of London and has been the bridge to other contacts further afield. I have been privileged to visit practising teachers and to work with others involved in this area of culture and education. In preparing this resource book for the busy teacher I hope also to have made a small offering to harmonious living at the present time.

JEAN GILBERT 1986

4

Contents

Key to notes for song melodies

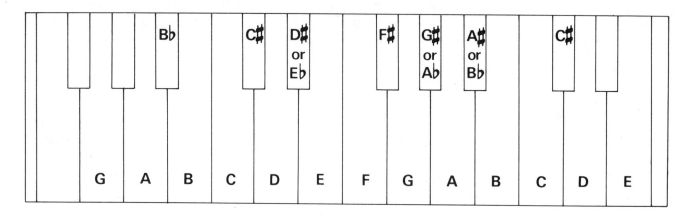

Piano

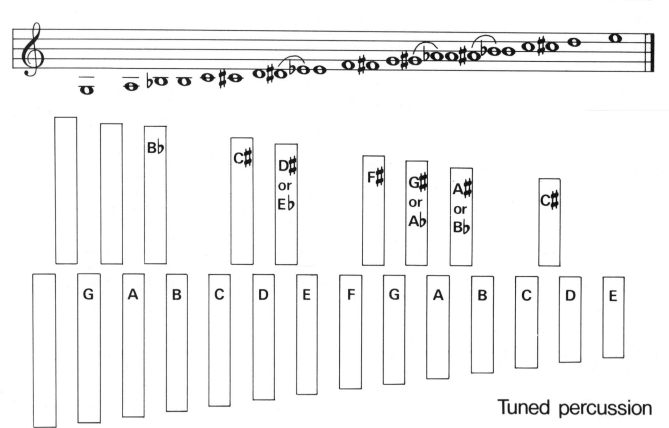

Tuned percussion

Learning the songs

The cassette accompanying this anthology will help teachers and children to learn the tunes.

The above chart provides further help for teachers where necessary. It includes all the notes of all the songs and can be used with both the piano and tuned percussion. The alto xylophone gives the same pitch as the piano. Smaller (soprano) instruments will give the same tune but at a higher pitch.

Tuned percussion accompaniments

Refer to the song pages.

♯ is the *sharp* symbol. It indicates a sound slightly *higher* than the named note.

♭ is the *flat* symbol. It indicates a sound slightly *lower* than the named note.

6

Background information

Harvest Festival comes at a time when the school year has just begun, when many children are getting used to a new classroom, the teacher, perhaps to a new group, and when the very youngest will be experiencing their first taste of going to school. It is partly for these reasons that it is probably not one of the most important festivals in the school year. However, this festival, rooted in the very basis of our survival, the production of food, would seem to offer a very suitable and important background for the children's activities in September and the beginning of October. For many children, especially those whose only experience of food may be of polythene-clad vegetables, frozen chicken carcasses and the magic pint on the doorstep every morning, an opportunity to learn about the background of this festival will help them appreciate its significance.

The celebrating of harvest dates back to pre-Christian times; the success of the harvest governed the lives of the people and their domestic animals and a good gathering of the crops was a very important event. The first sheaf of corn cut by the Saxon farmers was offered to one of their fertility gods to safeguard a good harvest the following year.

The last sheaf of corn was thought to house the Spirit of the Corn; it was feared that the spirit would die when this was cut unless an animal was sacrificed, so often a hare caught hiding in the corn was killed. Later a model of a hare made from straw from the last sheaf ensured that the Spirit of the Corn remained alive. Later still, a Corn Dolly (known variously as Corn or Kern Baby, Harvest Queen, the Mare or the Neck) was made from this last sheaf and tied to the rafters in the farmhouse until the next year. The reapers still didn't like the responsibility of cutting the last sheaf and often did it together by throwing their sickles at it from some distance away.

After a harvest supper a great deal of merry-making went on. In the Middle Ages the farmer and his family and relatives gave thanks to God in their local church before the supper; afterwards a 'Lady of the Harvest' was chosen from the local girls to grace the celebrations. It was not until 1843 that the tradition of organizing Harvest Thanksgiving Festival services began in churches. A successful service was held by Robert Hawker, vicar of Morwenstow in Cornwall, and the custom gradually spread.

Art and craft

Leaf printing

The gathering of the falling autumn leaves is a favourite occupation with children of all ages; activities with a class collection will vary according to the children but the most popular one is leaf printing:

Paint the *back* of a leaf – the veins show this side – then place the leaf, painted side downwards, on to white or whatever paper selected for the print. Cover with a double sheet of newspaper and press firmly over the covered leaf. Small hands may need to press several times over the entire leaf, or a roller could be used. Take away the newspaper and leaf and hang to dry.

Autumn fruit animals

Gather as many different types of cones, nuts and seed heads as you can; a walk in a local park or woody area will enable all children to participate. Let the children make drawings; encourage them to *look carefully* first. Then use the cones, nuts and seeds for making small models. Assemble them on a craft table and provide a small collection of bits and pieces like felt, string, beads and some strong glue like Copydex. The children will no doubt have their own ideas of what they want to make but here are some suggestions to start you off:

Cut oval ears of brown felt and line with pink felt, using Copydex. Stick the eyes about a third of the way between the tip of the cone and the ears, and stick the tail to the end of the cone. Rub a little paste onto the tip of the tail and taper it between the fingers.

Cut about an inch off the thick end of a fir cone with garden secateurs for the tortoise shell. A child can do the rest. The Rudbeckia seeds need painting with paste first to stop them falling to pieces as they dry out. When the paste is dry they can be stuck in position. The acorn head with two small beads eyes completes the animal.

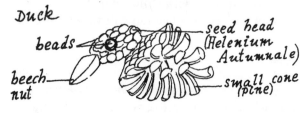

Assemble with glue as shown.

Ideas gathered from *Making Things Together* by Kathleen Douet and Valerie Jackson – Pelham Books 1973.

Corn dollies

Children will be fascinated to see some of these 'dollies', especially if you explain their background. There are many different traditional shapes, most of which are far too complicated for young children to attempt. However, if you can get some ripe oat, barley or wheat straws older infants will enjoy handling them and plaiting them into a simple shape. The stalks should be soaked for about two hours – to make them pliable – and raffia, wool or thick cotton can be used for tying. Traditionally many 'dollies' were finished with a red ribbon bow.

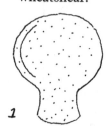

Festival food

Making bread

No amount of talking, looking at pictures, telling stories ('Little Red Hen') can rival the thrill of baking with yeast, handling the dough and smelling the smell of a fresh bake!

Yeast as a raising agent – a simple experiment
Put a little yeast with a pinch of sugar and a teaspoon of warm water into a test tube. Mix by shaking and stretch the neck of a balloon over the top. Patience should be rewarded by the sight of the balloon inflating as the yeast begins to ferment.

Use a standard recipe for your baking session. The children could make tiny loaves, rolls, animals or individual contributions to a harvest wheatsheaf.

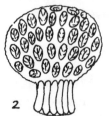

1 Make a sufficiently large base to accommodate the topping. Lift onto a lightly oiled baking tray and prick all over to prevent it rising too much. Cover.

2 Decorate with ears of grain and stalks. For the ears, form small pieces of dough into oval shapes, snip with scissors twice on each side, twice in the middle and attach to the base.

3 Make a plait, flatten with a rolling pin and secure over the top of the stalks. Complete the wheatsheaf with a harvest mouse. Eggwash the entire loaf, leave to rise slightly then bake for 30 to 45 minutes at 425°F (210°C), gas mark 7.

You now have an attractive addition to your Harvest display.

School Harvest Festival display

This is an ideal opportunity to develop the children's sense of colour and form in display, as well as giving them a time to really appreciate fresh fruit, vegetables, fish and good bread. Involve them in the early preparations.

1 Let the children write their own invitations to parents and friends to attend the festival.

2 Encourage them to present their gifts attractively. Talk about ways of doing this. Let them decorate boxes and other suitable containers one or two weeks beforehand.

3 Make a small classroom display the week before; include fresh fish bought on the day. What flowers are growing at this time of year?

Let each class have an unhurried opportunity of looking at the festival display before it is dismounted.

Musical activities

Movement

A lot of movement, especially with younger children, will be based on aspects of harvest and the onset of autumn and will be linked with singing games like 'Look at us and watch us'. Children living in urban areas may not have had the opportunity to observe or join in with these activities, so movement should be related to local activities like sweeping up leaves, raking grass (local parks or squares), picking up conkers, working on town or school allotments, or even shopping in the supermarket.

Link the movement with the action words:

Digging (potatoes)	firm downward arm movements; use the foot to lever up the earth then pick the potatoes
Raking (grass)	slow rhythmic pulling and pressing movements with the rake; tidy up the bundle of leaves and cart away
Picking (apples)	reaching high and low; picking carefully and putting in a basket; climbing a ladder
Sweeping (pavements)	slow movement lighter than raking; sweep leaves into a pile and put in cart
Cutting (flowers)	hold the flower and snip; gather a bundle and put in vase
Tossing (hay)	sticking the pitchfork into the hay and carefully lift and toss – the hay is heavy!
Stacking (sheaves)	gathering the bundle and tying up (now done by the combine harvester and the bailing machine)
Baking (bread)	mixing and kneading; putting in the oven
Shopping (supermarket)	searching the shelves; wheeling the trolley, paying at the check-out

Most children enjoy a guessing game so you could finish a movement session with individual children performing an action for the others to guess, using the correct action word. It is suggested that this movement is done unaccompanied at first.

Sound pictures

Now encourage the children to interpret these movements through sound. They will need to think about the kind of sound that would suggest the quality of the movements. Then they could sequence their sounds to convey the various movements that are part of each action:

	suggested percussion
Digging	*drum* or *tambour* (beat(s), scratch, tap(s))
Raking	*sand block* (slow scrapes, quick scrapes, taps)
Picking	*xylophone* (high and low notes for high/low

	movements stepwise up and down for climbing)	
Sweeping	*shaker* (long shakes, short shakes, taps)	
Cutting	*clappers* (taps and scrapes)	
Tossing	*tambourine* (tap and shake)	
Baking	*shaker* (shaking, tapping, scraping)	

Let each child or each group work out a repeat pattern. Hear them play one after another. When the patterns are well established choose about four. This could involve the whole group or a few children depending upon the instruments available. Now set two patterns going at the same time; add another one if this works, then all four can play together. Stop them one by one. Keep a first attempt very simple. (See also, the sound picture accompanying the song 'Autumn is here.')

Music corner

Mount pictures or the children's drawings to illustrate all the activities you have featured in the movement and music sessions, and leave out a selection of instruments that were used.

Sound pictures

Let the children practise the sound patterns introduced in the music session and relate them to one of the pictures or drawings. Two children could work together each choosing a different picture to interpret. They work one at a time then try playing together.

Similarly, if you have worked at a sound picture about the park or woods, display a suitable picture, drawing or collage that will help the children to recall what they did. Make available a selection of instruments that were used and allow the children to work in twos or threes to practise working together. Listen out for some interesting results; ask the children to play back when you can.

Making up tunes

Choose a simple couplet from one of the poems (better still – one written by the children) and introduce this activity with your class or group first:

1 Say the words rhythmically several times.
2 Clap and say the words.
3 Clap and whisper the words.
4 Now play a tune on the chime bars based on that rhythm.
5 Ask the children to sing the tune.
6 Let a few children have a turn; always sing the tune.

Prepare a simple work card and leave by the chime bars in the music corner for children to try their own tunes:

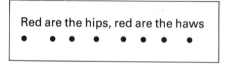

Tune using notes E G A

Playing by ear

Suitable 'snippets' for the children to try are outlined in the following songs:

Picking up conkers
I can see cherries
Autumn is here
This world goes round and round

It is important that the children know the tune well and can sing it before they start to play it in the music corner. Play it to them first and show them how to start. Prepare a simple work card as suggested in the song notes.

Picking up conkers

Melody by Geoffrey Russell-Smith
Words by Mollie Russell-Smith

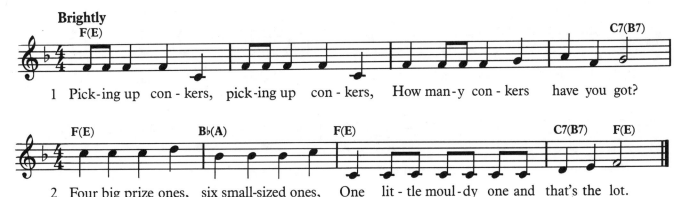

1 Pick-ing up con-kers, pick-ing up con-kers, How man-y con-kers have you got?

2 Four big prize ones, six small-sized ones, One lit-tle moul-dy one and that's the lot.

2 Picking up acorns, picking up acorns,
   How many acorns have you got?
   Five good green ones, four old brown ones,
   One little wormy one and that's the lot.

3 Picking up fir cones, picking up fir cones,
   How many fir cones have you got?
   Three fat round ones, two old squashed ones,
   One big enormous one and that's the lot.

Ask the children to draw pictures of the conkers, acorns and fir cones as a number activity and to write down the numbers. Adapt, if necessary, to the stage of number your children have reached.

Underline this link with number by asking the children to clap the number at the end of each verse.

Playing by ear

Ask the children to listen to the low note when you sing 'Picking up conkers'. Sing again and shape with your hands, moving well down for the syllable 'kers'. Play the two notes F and low C on a xylophone (chime bars if you have them) and let the children watch as your beater moves down to the A. Put in the music corner for the children to try, removing all the notes except F and C. Link with language by providing a simple work card:

```
Picking up conkers
F  F    F    F  C
```

Look at us and watch us

Nigerian schoolchildren's song by Akon Udonwa.
Words adapted by Elizabeth Singleton

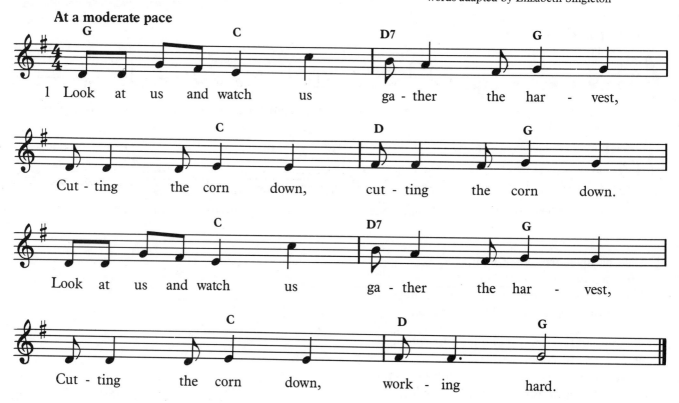

At a moderate pace

1 Look at us and watch us ga-ther the har-vest,
Cut-ting the corn down, cut-ting the corn down.
Look at us and watch us ga-ther the har-vest,
Cut-ting the corn down, work-ing hard.

2 Look at us and watch us gather the harvest,
  Picking the apples, picking the apples.
  Look at us and watch us gather the harvest,
  Picking the apples, working hard.

Adapt this attractive work song to the various
harvests that your children know about. These
could include 'pulling the nets in', 'digging
potatoes', 'driving the harvester', 'digging the coal
up' . . ., etc. Let them choose suitable percussion
to match the movements.

Singing game

The children walk or skip in a circle then stop to do
the work movements on lines two and four.
Alternatively, choose a small group of children to
'work' in the centre while everyone else skips or
walks round singing the song.

I can see cherries

Wendy van Blankenstein

Leisurely

VERSE

1 I can see cher - ries high up in the tree,

And there's a black - bird, he's sing - ing to me.

Come let's eat cher - ries, One, two, three, four,

Shake the tree, shake the tree, I'd like some more.

CHORUS

One, two, three, four, five, six, seven, eight, nine, ten,

One, two, three, four, five, six, seven, eight, nine, ten.

2 Let's collect conkers all shiny and brown,
   Look for the prickles that fall to the ground,
   Scuff the leaves over, so crispy and gold,
   Pick up the conkers, they're lovely to hold.

Adapt the first verse for younger children so that
they can sing about all the fruit trees that they
know: 'I can see apples/ripe pears/red plums high
up in the tree'. Add the minimum of percussion –
shakers for 'shake the tree . . .' and sticks or
clappers for the chorus.

   A more suitable pitch for this age would be key
E. **Guitar** chords would then be E   B   B7.

Suggested percussion (older children)

lines 1   2   3 triangle/Indian bells/finger cymbals

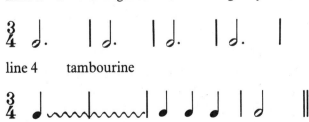

line 4   tambourine

Sticks or clappers can be used to mark the
'counting' throughout the chorus and in line 3 of
the verse.

Autumn is here

Margery Brinkmann, adapted by Jean Gilbert

Briskly

1 Au - tumn is here and the leaves are all chang - ing,
Red and yel - low and rus - set and brown.

Faster

Plums and cher - ries, nuts and ber - ries, Ap - ples and pears,

Slower

Au - tumn is here.

2 Autumn is here and the strong winds are blowing,
Tossing the tree tops and chasing the clouds.
Scamp and scurry, rush and hurry,
Tumble and toss!
Autumn is here.

3 Autumn is here and the squirrels all gather
Lots of nuts for the cold winter days.
Hear them chatter, field mice patter,
Moles creep away,
Autumn is here.

4 Autumn is here and the harvest is gathered,
Oats for porridge and wheat for our bread.
Thank you God for fruit and nuts
And vegetables too,
(Autumn is here.) Thanks for our food.

Concentrate on the words of this attractive harvest song. There is an interesting change of time half way through; a small fairly strong singing group could sing the third and fourth lines with everyone joining in with the last line 'Autumn is here'.

Optional accompaniment

lines 1 and 2 (chime bars or glock)

lines 3 and 4

line 5

Playing by ear

Sing the first line to the children and point out the 'jump' in the tune between the words 'is' and 'here'. Show them how to draw the pattern of the tune in the air:

Now show them how to play the first six notes of the tune and help them to finish the first line by providing a simple work card:

> Autumn is here and the leaves are all changing
> D   D D A   A A B   A G A F♯

The second line has the same tune.

Sound picture (younger children)

This activity can be associated with a visit to a local park or woody area. Encourage the children occasionally to stand very still and just listen. Let them listen to one another as they scuff through dried leaves or bracken or as they walk across the grass. Tape record 'woody' sounds, people walking in the wood perhaps a squirrel if you are lucky/ patient. Parents or older children might help provide other recordings.

The song *'Autumn is here'* will suggest 'sound' groups for the children, or choose groups according to their own suggestions.

Groups	Suggested sound makers
Wind	Voices sh . . . mm . . . ff . . .
Leaves	Shakers/sand blocks
Squirrels	Clappers/sticks/tissue paper being crumpled
Field mice	Quiet voices *eeeeeeee* . . . plus quiet rustle of paper
Birds	Bells/or some good whistlers/or recorders
People walking	Sand blocks/crumpled paper

Get a child to suggest an arrangement. One suggestion made to me was to represent people walking through a wood and play the sounds that they heard every time that they stopped to listen. So the wind and leaves provided a fairly continuous background against which we played: footsteps – squirrels – footsteps – birds – footsteps – field mice – footsteps getting quieter as the people go home – wind and leaves.

Fishermen

Music by Pauline Buzzing, words by E.M. Stockham

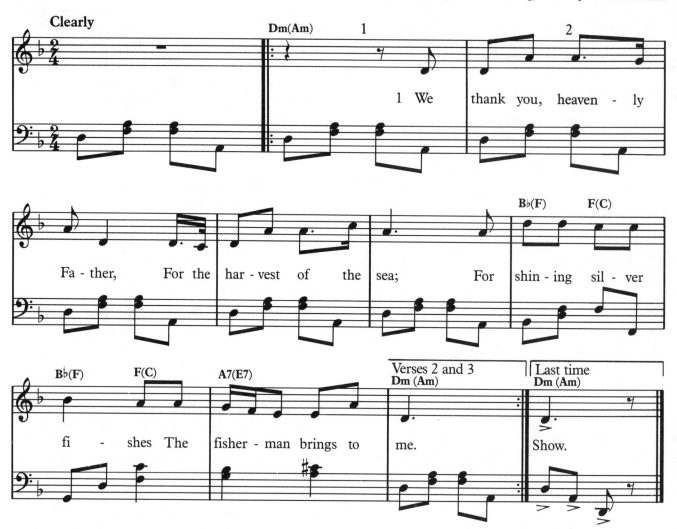

2 In wind and rain and sunshine,
   As they trail their long, brown nets,
   The small boats leave the harbour
   Just as the red sun sets.

3 Oh keep them safe, we pray You,
   When the stormy breezes blow,
   And bring them back at day-break
   With fine, full nets to show.

Sing this thanksgiving song very clearly, concentrating on the words. The middle verse could be sung as a round for older children (see parts 1 and 2 indicated in the music). Keep the rhythm steady and the singing quiet and clear.

Recorder

Play through as an introduction, accompany the singing or join the singing as the second part of a round.

Guitar is easier in Am (chords in brackets) – capo behind fifth fret. To sing in a lower key for younger children capo behind second or third fret.

Harvest in the city

Jane Morgan

Gaily, in calypso style

CHORUS

Har-vest time, it's har-vest time, Sum-mer's turn-ing to har-vest time.

Har-vest time, it's har-vest time, Best time of the year. *Fine*

VERSE

1 Ci-ties har-vest in fac-tor-y ___ Mak-ing things for you and me, ___

D.C. al Fine

Big ma-chines har-vest all the day, ___ This is the ci-ty way. ___

2 Stacking, packing in factory
Sending things for you and me,
Busy lorries are on the road
Bringing their harvest load.
CHORUS

3 Supermarket and local store,
We can find what we're shopping for.
Push round a trolley, pay at the till,
Here are the bags to fill.
CHORUS

Suggested percussion

Maracas in the chorus:

Chime bars or glockenspiel can accompany the melody in the verses:

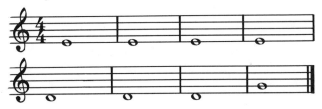

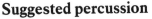

World harvest

Chorus melody and words by Richard Graves and Cecily Taylor,
adapted by Jean Gilbert
Verse melody by Jean Gilbert

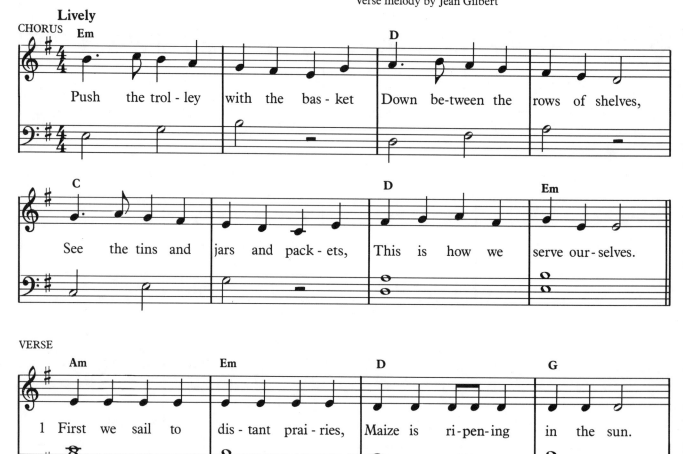

CHORUS

Push the trol-ley with the bas-ket Down be-tween the rows of shelves,
See the tins and jars and pack-ets, This is how we serve our-selves.

VERSE

1 First we sail to dis-tant prai-ries, Maize is ri-pen-ing in the sun.
Rea-dy for our bowls of corn-flakes When a-no-ther day's be-gun.

CHORUS

2 Let's steer on to warm Jamaica
  Pick bananas from the trees,
  See the canes and get our sugar,
  Then sail on across the seas.

CHORUS

3 Next stop - beef from Argentina,
  Coffee beans - Brazil ahead!
  Round the world we find New Zealand,
  There's the butter for our bread.

CHORUS

4 Now we travel on to China,
  Think of puddings made of rice;
  We'll collect some tea from India,
  Don't forget to find the spice.

CHORUS

5 Greece will have some dried sultanas,
  Currants, too, to fill our cakes,
  Pineapples from Africa and
  Lemons by Italian lakes.

CHORUS

6 Tinned sardines in Portugal, and
  Juicy oranges from Spain,
  Grapes from France and cheese from Holland,
  Then we'll sail for home again.

CHORUS

7 Rosy apples in the orchards,
  New - laid eggs must not be missed,
  Vegetables from market gardens,
  Now we've ticked off all our list.

CHORUS

8 Well, our trolley's really loaded,
  What a busy shopping day,
  Seems we needed all the world, and
  Now there's just the bill to pay.

Be selective with all these verses. A good idea would
be to start with two and build up according to the
interest of your group.

Suggested percussion

Tambourine in the chorus:

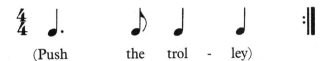

(Push   the   trol - ley)

This world goes round and round

Tom Paxton, adapted by Jean Gilbert

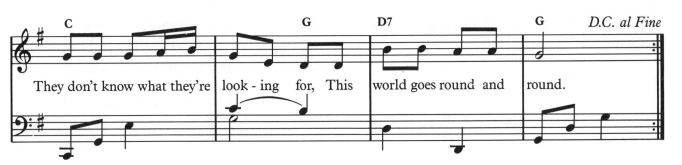

These words underline the inevitable cycle of the seasons and, while making no direct reference to harvest, might cause older children to consider the implications of today's harvests, of the sharing of food and of the 'haves' and 'have-nots'.

The shape of this arrangement is Chorus, Verse, Chorus. The song could be extended by singing the verse and chorus again. The verse should be sung slightly slower and very clearly.

Optional accompaniment

An alto xylophone will give a good sound but any tuned instrument can be used.

Suggested percussion

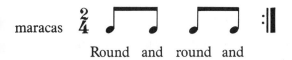

maracas

Round and round and

Playing by ear

The verse contains some interesting musical imitation. The second line has the same rhythmic and melodic pattern as the first but starts on a lower note.

Show the children how the first line can be played on four notes G A B C′:

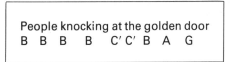

People knocking at the golden door
B B B   B   C′ C′ B A G

Now see if they can play the second line on notes F♯ G A B, starting on A.

More songs for Harvest time

Sing-a-Song One and Sing-a-Song Two
(Nelson)

Both these books have good sections with material for the younger child.

Book One
I'm a dingle dangle scarecrow
Old Macdonald had a farm
Harvest (song)
Oats and beans and barley grow (singing game)
The Harvest Festival (action song)

Book Two
The farmer's work (song and story)
The little red hen (story accompanied by a song)
Kum Ba Yah with adapted words:
    We've brought bags of flour at harvest time . . .
    We've brought loaves of bread at harvest time . . .

New Child Songs (Denholm House Press)

Here are more songs for younger children:
    See the farmer sow the seed
    Daily bread
    Autumn leaves
    God's care in winter (about leaves, birds and hedgehogs)

A Festival for Autumn
by Anne Mendoza (Novello)

This collection presents ten items for 'dramatic presentation or concert performance'. The following songs are relevant to this festival:
    Welcome to Autumn
    Autumn weather
    The apple tree
    The Harvest song
    Jimmy the scarecrow

'Look for signs that summer's done'
from *Someone's singing, Lord* (A. & C. Black)

This song has attractive lyrics that would appeal to the older child and a 'broadness' about it that makes it suitable for an assembly or Harvest Festival. The piano accompaniment is simple but very supportive musically and the tune goes well on descant recorders.

'Indian harvest'
from *Topic Anthologies for Young Children* Book 2 (O.U.P.)

This is a most beautiful song rooted in North American Indian music and underlines the universal importance of harvest.

Harvest Time
by Kenneth Pont (O.U.P.)

An anthology of music and verse for infant and junior schools arranged for voices, recorders, tuned percussion and piano.

Turnip Head
by Jan Holdstock (Universal)

This booklet comprises a group of lively songs and activities for the autumn.

'Paint-box'
by V.P. and H.C. Mitchell from *Harlequin* (A. & C. Black)

This song will enliven any occasion with its catchy tune and topical words all about fruit and vegetables. Older children will enjoy it all and even younger children can join in straight away with the chorus:

    The apples are ripe, the plums are red,
    Broad beans are sleeping in a blankety bed.

Also in this collection is a song about seeds popping and one about the fog.

Seasonal hymns

Hymns for older children available in standard hymn books:
    We plough the fields and scatter
    Come, ye thankful people, come
    Let us with a gladsome mind

Poems

Bread

'Farmer, is the harvest ready
  For we must have bread?'
'Go and look at all my fields,'
  Is what the farmer said.

So we ran and saw the wheat
  Standing straight and tall.
'There's your bread,' the farmer said,
  'Have no fear at all.'

'Miller, is the flour ready
  For we must have bread?'
'Go and look in all my sacks.'
  Is what the miller said.

So we ran and saw the flour,
  Soft and white as snow.
'There's your flour,' the miller said,
  As we turned to go.

'Mother, is the oven ready
  For we must have bread?'
'Go and open wide the door,'
  Is what our mother said.

So we ran and saw the loaves
  Crisp and brown to see.
'There's your bread,' our mother said,
  'Ready for your tea.'

          H.E. Wilkinson

This poem lends itself to group speaking, either in
two groups for the two halves of each verse for
younger children, or in groups for the children's
questions and the narrative, with individual
children for the farmer, the miller and the mother.

Harvest home

Wheat is all cut,
Oats safe in bags,
Barley just ripe,
Tractor zig-zags
Bumping downhill
Trailer with beans
And at the wheel
Girl in blue jeans.
In orchard below,
Baskets of plums
Wait under trees
Till fruit lorry comes
To take them away.
Harvest is in.
And home go the growers,
The pickers, the mowers;
Let dancing begin
At end of day
Now harvest is in.

          Leonard Clark

The winged seed

The winged seed from the sycamore
Flutters down like propellers of a helicopter.
Walking through a park
You see the old people shivering
On a park bench.
Look up, you see geese
Flying south into the sun.

          Cathy Collier
   William Tyndale School, London

Autumn

Yellow the bracken,
Golden the sheaves,
Rosy the apples,
Crimson the leaves;
Mist on the hillsides,
Clouds grey and white.
Autumn, good morning
Summer, good night.

Anon

Red in Autumn

Red are the hips, red are the haws,
Red and gold are the leaves that fall,
Red are the poppies in the corn,
Red berries on the rowan tall;
Red is the big round harvest moon,
And red are my new little dancing shoes.

Elizabeth Gould (Extract)

Vegetables

A carrot has a green fringed top,
    A beet is royal red,
And lettuces are curious
    All curled and run to head.

Some beans have strings to tie them on,
    And what is still more queer,
Ripe corn is nothing more or less
    Than one enormous ear!

But when potatoes all have eyes,
    Why is it they should be
Put in the ground and covered up –
    Where it's too dark to see?

Rachel Field

Autumn poem

Autumn, I think, is a funny time of year
As winter's coming in,
It rains a lot, and cars whizz by
They soak you to the skin.
The sky turns from blue to grey
The hours pass almost silently away
And all too soon the day is gone.

When you're in the city
You seem to be tucked away,
Hemmed inside the city walls
When the sun has gone astray.
Autumn brings mist and gloom
Filling every cheerful room,
Autumn brings a sense of mystery.

Farne Sinclair (age 10)
Canonbury Junior School, London

from Autumn

It is the football season once more
And the back pages of the Sunday papers
Again show the blurred anguish of goalkeepers.

In Maida Vale, Golders Green and Hampstead
Lamps ripen early in the surprising dusk;
They are furred like stale rinds with a fuzz of mist.

The pavements of Kensington are greasy;
The wind smells of burnt porridge in Bayswater,
And the leaves are mushed to silence in the gutter.

The big hotel like an anchored liner
Rides near the park; lit windows hammer the sky.
Like the slow swish of surf the tyres of taxis sigh.

It is a time of year that's to my taste,
Full of spiced rumours, sharp and velutinous flavours,
Dim with the mist that softens the cruel surfaces,
Makes mirrors vague. It is the mist that I most favour.

Vernon Scannell

A play with music

The story of Ruth

Teachers are referred to the full biblical story in the four chapters of the Book of Ruth.

Characters
Narrator
Naomi
Elimelech, Naomi's husband
Mahlon ⎱
Chilion ⎰ Naomi's sons
Ruth ⎱
Orpah ⎰ Naomi's daughters-in-law
Boaz, Naomi's relative
Reapers

Music
The opening bars of Handel's overture to *Judas Maccabeus* can be used to set the scene at the beginning and to accompany the first entry of Naomi and her family. The last part of this overture can be used at the end of the final scene. Alternatively, the children can improvise, (see suggestions on page 26).

Enter Narrator walking slowly. The narrator explains that there has been a very bad harvest in the land of Judah and that many people will starve because of lack of food. Exit.

Enter Naomi, her husband and two sons to quiet, subdued music. They are dejected. They talk about the lack of food resulting from the failure of the harvest and wonder what to do. Elimelech decides that they should leave Judah to settle in the country of Moab. They slowly pack up, collect all their goods and chattels and walk round on their journey (*slow drum or tambour beat*). Finally they stop and shield their eyes to peer into the distance (*cymbal*). Naomi says she can see their new country; they will go to start a new life. Exit to *brighter drum beat*.

Enter Narrator (*drum beat*) to explain that the family lived in Moab for ten years and that both sons married in that country. But when Naomi's husband and two sons died, Naomi wondered whether she should go back to her own country of Judah to join her relatives. Exit.

Enter Naomi, Ruth and Orpah (*slow drum beat*). Naomi tells her daughters-in-law of her plans and advises them to return to their own families. They talk about what they should all do. Ruth finally says that she will not leave Naomi. 'Where you go I will go, and where you lodge I will lodge; . . . where you die I will die and there will I be buried.' (*Book of Ruth*, Chapter 1: verses 16/17).
So Naomi and Ruth take their bundles, say goodbye to Orpah and exit. Orpah watches and slowly exits the other side (*drum beat*).

Enter Reapers and prepare to work as Naomi and Ruth enter slowly. They are tired after their long journey but are pleased to have reached Judah. The reapers wonder who the two women are. One of them recognizes Naomi. The latter introduces Ruth, her daughter-in-law from Moab, and explains that she has come back to Judah because her husband and two sons have died. They go on their way. The reapers grumble that because Ruth is a foreigner she cannot expect to share their food. She has come at the time of the barley harvest but the food they reap must last them until the next harvest. They exit grumbling.

Enter Naomi and Ruth discussing their future. Ruth asks if she may go gleaning to gather the fallen stalks from among the sheaves. Naomi advises her to stay in the field of Boaz, her kinsman. Exit.

Enter the reapers who get down to work. They cut the barley and stack it in sheaves. (This action can be accompanied by *clappers*, *shakers* and *sand blocks*.) Enter Ruth with a bag slung over her shoulder. She begins to pick up some fallen stalks. The reapers are unfriendly. Enter Boaz who asks who the young gleaner is. The reapers reply that she is a Moabite woman. Boaz knows about her devotion to Naomi. He welcomes her to his field and says that she is to be treated just like the other workers, that she may eat and drink with them all. He also advises his reapers to make sure there is plenty for her to glean. The work proceeds in a happier frame of mind. Ruth enters and Naomi shows her how much she has gleaned. Boaz invites them back to his home. Exit to *recorded music* or children's improvisations.

Enter Narrator to tell the end of the story, that Ruth stayed with Naomi in Judah. Her kindness to Naomi had been rewarded and the people of Judah had learnt to be kind to strangers.

Children's improvisations

Sad music

Let the children improvise slowly using notes C D E F. *Descending* phrases will underline unhappiness:

chime bars, alto glockenspiel or metallophone

An alto or bass xylophone can accompany. A very slow beat will support the character of the music:

Happy music

Use a higher register and *ascending* notes. The children might find rhythms from a suitable verse helpful:

(See the rea - pers work - ing hard, Ruth has come to glean.)

(Work a while and rest a while, Hap - py har - vest team!) J.G.

Use any tuned instruments except ones giving a really low sound. Accompany with bells or a tambourine.

Background information

Sukkot, also known as the Festival of Tabernacles, is a Jewish festival that marks the gathering of the Autumn harvest. It recalls God's protection of the Israelites during their wanderings in the Wilderness, when they lived in temporary dwellings over a long period described as forty years.

The festival's origin can be seen in *Leviticus* (23) 'Ye shall dwell in booths seven days . . .' Many families build a little hut called a **sukkah** on their gardens or balconies to remind them of God's protection during those historic wanderings. The roof is made of branches and leaves with sufficient spaces for the stars to be seen through as a symbol of God's continuing protection. The sukkah is decorated with leaves and fruit and here meals are taken during the eight-day festival. The first two days are the most important. Schools are closed, no ordinary work is done and Synagogue services are longer and more colourful. After that, normal working days are resumed but families continue to sit and eat in the sukkah and to say special prayers.

During the festival blessings are made to God with a symbolic selection of leaves and fruit known as the **Four Species**:

Lulav – the shoot of a young palm tree
Etrog – a citron (large lemon)
Hadas – myrtle leaves
Arava – willow leaves

During the synagogue service the **Torah**, the holy scroll containing the Law or 'teachings' of the Jews, is taken out of the Ark and carried in procession to the accompaniment of singing and dancing.

I will plant in the wilderness the cedar,
The acacia tree, and the myrtle, and the oil tree;
I will set in the desert, the cypress, the plane tree, and the larch together;
That they may see, and know and consider and understand together,
That the hand of the Lord hath done this,
And the Holy One of Israel hath created this.

Isaiah, Chapter 41, verses 18/20

Art and craft

Posters

Paint or draw posters showing the *Four Species*. If possible produce the real leaves and a large lemon or show the children some good illustrations.

Models

Model life-size fruit and vegetables from papier mâché.

METHOD:

1 Tear up newspaper into small pieces, about 3 cm.

2 Assemble in a bucket and add about three tablespoons of paste and enough water to just soak the paper.

3 Stir well and leave until suitable for kneading, about two days.

4 Squeeze the water out thoroughly, then knead and shape into models. Leave for 24 hours or longer until dry.

5 Paint and varnish. Use for display or to decorate a sukkah model.

Leaf prints

Paint the back of a leaf, cover with paper and press firmly to get an impression. Use as required.

Mobiles

Use models or drawings of the *Four Species*.

Sukkah models

1 Use a shoe box or cardboard carton. Cut windows and a door and paint or cover with leaves and twigs. Decorate with small models or drawings of fruit. Cut away or turn on one side so that a family can be seen taking a meal inside. Use dolls, house furniture or make matchbox furniture and pipe-cleaner dolls.

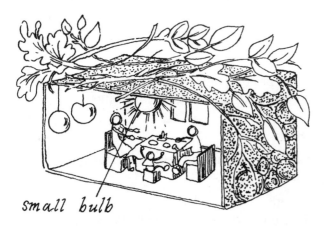

small bulb

2 Use an old umbrella: a child's one would be suitable. Remove the cloth and weave twigs through the skeleton frame letting some leafy parts hang down over the sides. Insert into a firm base such as the ground, plaster of paris, large flower pot filled with compressed earth or similar container filled with discarded plasticine. Hang little models of fruit from the umbrella and seat dolls or puppets underneath.

Festival food

There are no special dishes served at Harvest Festival time; the one most likely to be on the menu is Stuffed Cabbage. This is made with large white cabbage leaves which are softened in boiling water, filled with a mixture of rice, meat, onion and seasoning and rolled up and secured with string like a parcel. They are then cooked on a bed of cabbage leaves with tomato puree, water, raisins and sugar for about two hours.

The rest of the menus will include favourite dishes like **gefillte** or fried fish, chicken soup, boiled or roast chicken, strudel and honey cake. Jewish dietary laws forbid the mixing of milk and meat and in orthodox families milk and meat dishes are never served at the same meal. In addition, meat is only permitted from animals that have the cloven hoof and chew the cud; fish must have fins and scales. The slaughter of animals and killing of poultry must be done according to Jewish humane ritual killing and must be further prepared (*kashered*) for the housewife.

Happy Festival   Yom Tov Lanu

Hebrew folk song, translated by Reuben Turner
English lyrics by Jean Gilbert

Come and join us in our suk-kah For it is our fes-ti-val, A
Yom tov la-nu chag sa-me-ach y'-la-dim na-gi-la na L'

hap-py time for all the chil-dren, A hap-py day for the fa-mi-ly.
su-ka-te-nu ba o-re-ach Av-ra-ham a-vi-nu ba-ruch ha-ba.

Wel-come Ab-ra-ham, Ab-ra-ham our fa-ther comes.
Ya had et-ha-chag-na-chog b'-lu-lav ha-das et-rog Ba

-day we sing and dance,____ To-day we sing and dance.
ma a gal nir-kod,____ Ba ma a gal nir-kod.

Suggested percussion

tambour or bongo drum

tambourine

Dance movements

Any number of children in a circle:

Bars 1–4 Join hands, take seven jaunty walking steps to the left and stop.

Bars 5–8 Seven walking steps back to the right and stop.

Bars 9–10 Four steps into the middle raising arms.

Bars 11–12 Four steps back again lowering arms.

Bars 13–14 Clap hands.

Bars 15–16 Skip round on the spot.

With hammer and nails Patish Masmer

Music by N. Nardi, words by Harousi
translated by Rita Kalev

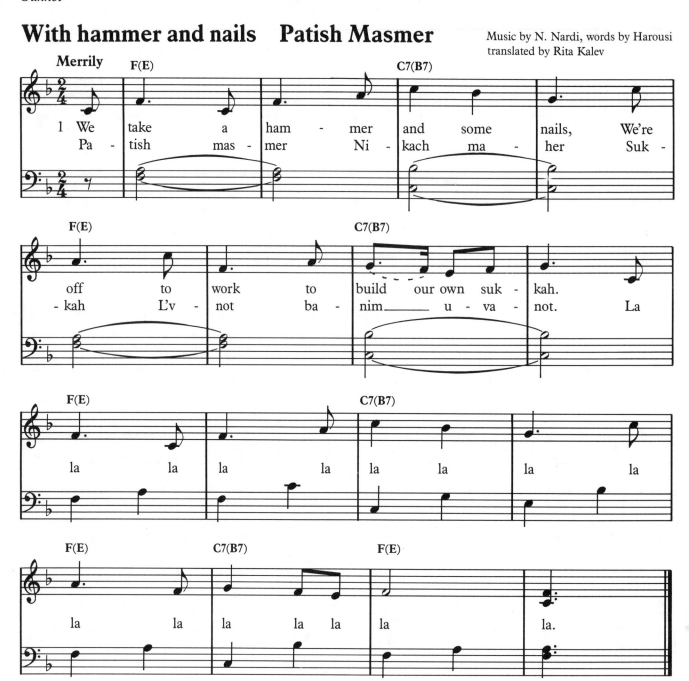

Merrily

1 We take a ham - mer and some nails, We're
Pa - tish mas - mer Ni - kach ma - her Suk -

off to work to build our own suk - kah.
- kah L'v - not ba - nim u - va - not. La

la la la la la la la

la la la la la la la.

2 With hammer and saw we chisel away,
We work so hard, we're busy all the day.
La la la . . .

Ask your children in what other ways they would
work to build a sukkot and make up some more
verses with them around these actions.

Sing and dance in a circle, moving on the first two
lines of the verse and stopping to mime the actions
on the 'las'. These can be repeated if you want to
sustain the movement.

Suggested percussion

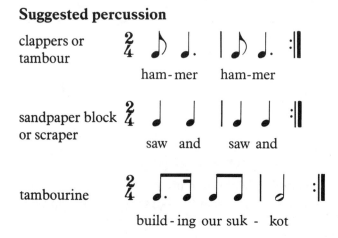

clappers or
tambour

ham - mer ham - mer

sandpaper block
or scraper

saw and saw and

tambourine

build - ing our suk - kot

Background information

The Eve of All Hallows, or Hallowe'en as we know it, falls on October 31st. It is the prelude to All Saints' Day, November 1st and All Souls' Day, November 2nd. These three days are together known as **Hallow Tide**.

Coming a few weeks after the end of the Harvest season, it marks the end of the good weather and the beginning of the long winter nights. In Celtic times it marked the beginning of another year and was celebrated with a Festival of Fire. The lighting of fires around the villages symbolized the power of the sun, purified the empty fields and helped to keep out witches and evil spirits that were traditionally supposed to be around at this time. People also hung up lanterns made from large turnips or pumpkins, spread salt around keyholes to keep out spies and threw salt over their shoulders to ward off these creatures of the dark. Masks were worn to prevent recognition by spirits which, it was thought, passed into the bodies of animals; nicknames were used for the same reason.

Many other superstitions have been associated with Hallowe'en. Eating nuts was thought to be both a good protection against evil spirits and a means of acquiring wisdom. Eating apples ensured health in the New Year; a complete apple peel waved around the head of a young girl would indicate the initial letter of her future husband by the shape it formed when it dropped to the ground.

The time of Hallowe'en can stimulate much creative and imaginative work and if Harvest Festival celebrations are held reasonably early, sufficient time can be devoted to this interesting festival. Teachers of very young or sensitive children will be aware that they might be frightened by certain aspects of the supernatural, especially of the dark, and will plan their activities accordingly. Witches, for instance, can be funny, happy or helpful; their spells can go wrong with comical consequences! Another antidote is to encourage the children to play at being witches. Turn the home corner into a witch's den by draping some dark cloth over the frame of the Wendy house and darkening the windows with some coloured tissue paper, – blue, green or red. Make a secret entrance and hang up a notice 'Witch at home'. The children can decorate the inside with mysterious signs and symbols using glittery paper, and with very simple spiders made from pipe cleaners. There must be a 'cauldron' inside, some pretend jars of good/bad luck potions and a book of spells.

Art and craft

Wall frieze

Make a wall frieze stimulated by any of the witchy stories that the children have enjoyed. My children made a life-sized model of a witch and her cauldron. We stood them against the background of a witch's kitchen with hanging spiders' webs, slinking cats, pet frogs and watchful owls. Nearby was our music table so that the children could bring their gloomy kitchen to life with atmospheric sounds and musical spells.

A number frieze could be based on the poem 'Wild witches' ball'. There are 'ten tall crones', 'nine queer dears', 'eight witches with mangy tresses' and so on. Each child could contribute one or more witches for the frieze. With younger children just concentrate on the first and last verses and decide on your own number.

Witches

Children like to make their own witch models. If these are mounted on a twig broomstick they can 'fly' round the room or extend part of the frieze.

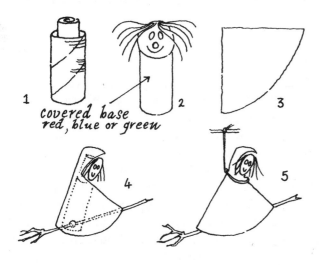

covered base
red, blue or green

1 Make the face and body from a toilet roll holder or squeezy container cut in half, plus rolled up newspaper. Cover with shiny paper.
2 Stick on a prepared face and some straw or wool hair.
3 Improvise a hood and cloak from a suitably large semi-circular piece of black tissue paper.
4 Secure a twig through the paper cloak and the bottom of the inside base.
5 Tie thick black cotton round neck and hang in a flying position.

The children will be interested to know that witches were at one time respected members of the community. They were able to use their knowledge of herbs and other plants to heal the sick. They kept many secrets of nature; some also knew about the moon and the stars. Their peculiar cone-shaped hats were typical of those worn by most women. Later on society turned against them and they were associated with evil and the supernatural. Older children might like to make a study of witches and of superstitions associated with Hallowe'en.

Witches' hats

Use black, green or red sugar paper, very thin card or anything else suitable for child-sized hats.

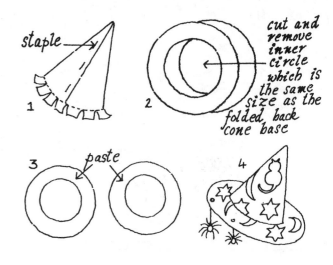

staple

cut and remove inner circle which is the same size as the folded back cone base

paste

1 Roll the paper into a cone to fit the child's head. Staple and trim to size. Cut around the bottom of the cone and fold back the cuts.
2 Cut two circles bigger than the base of the cone.
3 Paste one side of each circle and sandwich the flaps at the base of the cone in between.
4 Decorate the whole hat with stars, moons, cats, spiders and so on.

Masks

1 *Paper bags*
Thickish brown paper bags are one of the easiest types for young children. Put the bag over the head, mark the position of the eyes, nose and mouth. Remove, draw the desired shapes and cut out. Stick on 'hair', paint eyebrows and ears or turn into an animal by sticking on ears, whiskers and the like.

2 *Paper plates*
Mark the position of the eyes, nose and mouth, cut out, paint and decorate as desired. A box of junk containing scraps like wool, drinking

straws, crepe paper, egg boxes and sweet papers
is all that is needed.

3 *Eye masks*
Have mask bases ready prepared from suitable
card and let the children do the rest. They can cut
out eye shapes, add hair/ears/nose/big ears and
finally paint or decorate.

4 *Lanterns*
These can be made from large turnips or
pumpkins. They cannot be tackled by young
children and are best done by an adult – parent or
helper – in a small group with the children
watching and doing a bit of the scraping. Use the
opportunity to talk about the vegetables, shapes
and the background of Hallowe'en.

METHOD:
Cut off the top for a lid and scoop out the inside
with a suitable knife. Take care to leave a strong
'shell'. Cut out shapes for the eyes, nose and
mouth. Fix a handle of strong wire or other
suitable material. Finally put smoke holes into
the lid. A small dumpy candle or night light will
withstand movement the best.

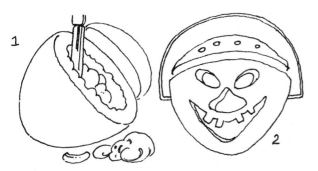

Musical activities

Movement

Whatever kind of dramatic or dance activity you
plan with the children it will be necessary to give
them some experience of basic movements that can
be applied to 'witchy' situations.

Witches and wizards
Slow slinky movements using a bent body, an
occasional twisty turn right round with arms
writhing and fingers curved and separated as if
knarled. The facial expression is very important.
The children can 'pull' as many weird faces as they
like, but they must sustain the particular type of
witch-like face they have chosen to concentrate on.
The eyes are also important. They can rove around,
dart from side to side, focus on one particular
corner or mesmerise someone or something.
Encourage a few hoarse cackles. See *Tune making,
Making up tunes*, 'Heigh-ho for Hallowe'en'
page 35.

The cauldron
Children find it difficult to fill and stir a cauldron –
it is usually all over in a few seconds! Help them to
describe what a cauldron might look like in reality,
how big it might be, how heavy, what it might be
made of, what the witch's brew might feel like when
stirred round. Use a large carton if necessary to give
an idea of size, put some bits and pieces in and let
them take turns stirring with a stick.

Filling the cauldron should be done with flourish
and ceremony. The ingredients should be handled
with caution and held high for everyone to see
before being dropped into the stew. All the
movements should be 'slow motion'.

Cats
The witch's cat will prowl, arch its back, hiss and
spit. Its movements can be unpredictable and
sinister. The children could easily interpret the
character moving on two legs – as distinct from 'all
fours' – for it could well be a human being disguised
as a cat.

Owls
These can fly and perch, fly and perch. The flying
wing movement in the arms should be a slow up and
down beat for this is a big bird. When the owl
perches the children could encircle their eyes with
their hands to indicate the large blinking eyes of the
owl. The head can turn slowly from side to side.

Listening

There are various activities included in the notes accompanying each song. See especially the listening and moving game to do with the song *The witch*.

Word rhythms

Let each child make up a short spell or chant. Choose about four and learn them. Prepare rhythm cards:

```
┌─────────────────────────────────────┐
│                                      │
│  Abracadabra stir and stir           │
│  •   •   •   •   •   •   •   •        │
│                                      │
└─────────────────────────────────────┘

┌─────────────────────────────────────┐
│                                      │
│  Hocus pocus honey pot               │
│  •   •   •   •   •   •   •            │
│                                      │
└─────────────────────────────────────┘
```

Use the symbol • for a clap or note. Work in this way:
1 *Read* the card several times concentrating on the rhythm of the words.
2 *Say* the words and *clap* rhythmically several times.
3 *Whisper* the words and *clap* rhythmically several times.
4 *Think* the words and *clap* rhythmically several times.
When the children can clap several cards, play the game 'Which one did I clap?' Whoever guesses correctly can have a turn at clapping, and so on.

The Spell game

Put the spells the children have learnt to clap in a 'cauldron'. The children sit on the ground in a circle with the cauldron in the middle. Place some chime bars, say D E G and A, together with a beater near the cauldron. Pass a wooden spoon round the circle while chanting:

> Round and round the spoon must go.
> Pass it on and we shall know
> Who will pick the magic spell,
> Who will choose and who will tell.

Whoever holds the spoon on the word 'tell' stirs the cauldron and picks out a spell. They choose one of the chime bars and play the spell. Everyone joins in singing it. The game continues. Later the spells could be written, decorated and placed in a class spell book.

The game is more successful if the children have been able to use the chime bars and the spells in the music corner beforehand.

Sound picture

A witch's kitchen	*Suggested sound makers*
the witch	voices laughing/cackling
the cauldron	
being stirred	sand block and shakers
bubbling	ripples on the xylophone
smoking	voices *ff-shsh-ff-shsh*
the spell	random notes on the chimes or glockenspiel
cats	voices *meeeooow*
bats	voices *eeeeee eeeeee*
frogs	clappers or wood block
spiders	gentle scrapes on guiro, rasp or washboard

Suggested arrangement
Let the group of children playing the 'cauldron' work out a pattern and play as a background all the time. The cats, bats, frogs and spiders can sound one after the other in any order. They will stop as the witch is heard. She makes several spells (the spell children have worked out a pattern) and goes out laughing. The cauldron bubbles away and finally dies down.
(Look also at the song 'Hallowe'en' and the poem 'Old Moll' for more suggestions for sound pictures.)

Music corner

When you have introduced rhythm cards in connection with spells (see *Listening activities*) leave them in the music corner together with instruments that are easy to play rhythmically. The children can work with a partner, one playing a card, the other guessing which card it was.

Making up tunes

Introduce this activity first with your class, using the rhythm cards you have prepared for their spells. Show younger children how to play the rhythm of a spell on one note – E or G – older children can use three or four notes according to their experience.

Using notes E and G

A - bra - ca -da - bra   stir and stir.

Using notes D E G A

Ho - cus   po - cus   ho - ney pot.

1 Clap the rhythm of the spell all together.
2 You play the rhythm on the chime bar(s) to be used.
3 The children sing the tune.
4 A few children have turns – always sing afterwards.

You can now leave the chime bars and the cards in the music corner as an activity for one or two children.

Older children or those more experienced at tune-making will enjoy 'setting' the following rhyme:

> Heigh-ho for Hallowe'en,
> All the witches to be seen,
> Some in black and some in green,
> Heigh-ho for Hallowe'en!

They could use all the notes C D E G A and possibly a B♭ instead of top C. To make their tune longer or more interesting they could repeat the first and last lines, repeating their tune as well. Link the tune(s) with your witch dance!

Playing by ear

Suitable snippets for the children to try are outlined in the notes to the following songs:

> The witch
> Witches of Hallowe'en
> Souling song
> Hallowe'en
> Hansel and Gretel

The children must listen carefully to the sound of the notes they are playing and relate them to the tunes they are remembering. It is important, therefore, that they know the tune well and can sing it before they start to play it on the chimes.

Sound pictures

When you have successfully produced a sound picture with a group leave out the instruments you have used in the music corner. Prepare a simple illustrated work card to remind them of what they did.

Liven up the music corner with the children's drawings, stories and paintings. This will all add to what they will produce in their own sound pictures.

The witch

Jean Gilbert

2 The wind is howling through the trees,
The sky is very black, (mysteriously)
Oo - oo, oo - oo,
Hallowe'en is back.

3 The cat is prowling through the grass,
Can you see her eyes? (quietly)
Meow - meow,
Catch her by surprise! (whisper)

4 The goblins dance and jump about,
Up and down the street, (jerkily)
Click clack, click clack,
Go their dancing feet.

Suggested percussion

 shakers/sand block played quietly throughout

 slow beat on a tambour – padded beater

 tambourine strike after last word

 clappers or castanets throughout

This song is suitable for younger children and will provide the basis for some dramatic movement. Make up some more verses with the children about their favourite Hallowe'en characters and ask the children to choose their own percussion.

Musical game

When the children know the song well and are familiar with the various instruments associated with each character, select three of their favourite ones and play them for the children to move to. The children could also work with a partner or in groups, one playing and the other(s) moving. Now develop the children's ability to listen and remember by hiding the instruments – a bookcase or similar screening will do.

1 Play the instruments one by one with silences in between. The children must move, then freeze into a statue of the character represented by the instrument when it stops playing.

2 Divide the children into three groups, each group choosing a different character to dance. The groups only move when they hear the instrument for their character playing. Occasionally play two instruments together – with help, of course. The children must listen carefully and move quietly for this.

Using chime bars

Leave out chimes D E F G A in the music corner and encourage the children to play up and down note by note. Some children will be able to play in the rhythm of the words, 'Riding in the sky' as they play *going up*, and of the words 'See her flashing by' as they play *going down*. Help them by clapping the words first. Play a game with a group asking them which line you have played; you play the chimes first and they sing the correct words.

Playing by ear

Three notes will enable the children to try the first line:

The witch is on her broomstick						
D	D	E F	E	D		D

With the addition of G and A they will be able to play up and down for the second and fourth lines and a B♭ will complete the sound of the 'oos'.

Recorders

This is a good tune for introducing B♭ with older children. If suitable, one or two recorders could accompany the song, playing just the two notes A   B♭ on the 'oos'. Once the B♭ has been mastered some children could play the tune right through.

Optional accompaniment

The following two-note tune will fit all the way through except for the 'oo' bars:

Play these bars on the chime bars or recorders:

(Oo - oo,   Oo - oo)

Witch watch

Jane Morgan

Dramatically

1 It's the witch, witch, witch - es that watch, watch, watch un -
til you go to bed. Then they zoom, zoom, zoom on their
broom, broom, brooms, Right a - bove your head.

CHORUS

Fly witch, _____ fly high, _____ Right a - bove our heads.

Fly witch, _____ Fly high, _____ While we dream in bed.

2 Then the witch, witch, witches
That watch, watch, watch
Fly down to make their spells.
Hear them whirr, whirr, whirr,
See them stir, stir, stir,
There in caves and dells.

Suggested percussion

 shakers

 sand blocks

 guiro

 scratched drum head

CHORUS

Fly witch, fly down,
Right above our heads.
Fly witch, fly down,
While we dream in bed.

3 See their tall, black hats,
   See their slinky cats,
   These witches of the night.
   See them twist and turn,
   See them cook and churn,
   Misty, magic sight.

   CHORUS

   Fly witch, fly high,
   Right above our heads.
   Fly witch, fly high,
   While we dream in bed.

 cymbal strikes – padded beater
 cymbal – quiet tremolo
cymbal strikes
cymbal – quiet tremolo

 guiro

 clappers

 tambourine

 as before

Optional accompaniments

xylophone (verse)

chime bars or glockenspiel (chorus)

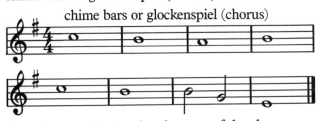

Recorders could also play the tune of the chorus.

Playing by ear

Start with the chorus. Show the children how to begin and leave notes G A B C′ in the music corner together with a simple work card:

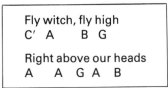

Fly witch, fly high
C′ A   B G

Right above our heads
A   A G A B

Movement

This song introduces the idea of witches in a dreamlike setting and a final dance arrangement could be built around this fantasy. Preparatory movement could include the witches as they watch and wait, as they mount their brooms and take off, as they fly down to their caves and as they busy themselves preparing and making spells. Other creatures like cats, bats and toads could be included.

Suggested arrangement
Choose a centre group of children for the 'dreamers'. They will sing and play percussion. The cats, bats and toads will move and mime in their caves and dells in a much larger circle well away from the singers. The witches will then dance around the central group.

Verse 1 The witches watch then mount their brooms and fly round. The creatures on the ground react to them.

Verse 2 The witches fly down and settle in their caves where they begin their magic spells aided by the creatures.

Verse 3 They continue their magic (slow motion movements are effective). Then they fly away on the final chorus. Everyone hums as the dreaming children finally settle.

Art

Let every child paint a large face of a witch, cut out the eyes and mount the faces on red, green or blue frieze paper.

Souling song

Traditional English

Clearly, at a steady pace

CHORUS

A soul, a soul, a soul cake! Please good mis-ses a soul cake! An

ap-ple, a pear, a plum or a cher-ry, A-ny good thing to make us all mer-ry,

One for Pe-ter, two for Paul, Three for Him who made us all.

VERSE

The lanes are ve-ry dir-ty, my shoes are ve-ry thin.____ I've____
have-n't got a pen-ny, a ha'-pen-ny will do.____ If you____

got a lit-tle po-cket to put a pen-ny in.____ If you
have-n't got a ha'-pen-ny, then God __ bless____ you.

In former times children and often grown-ups too would go out **souling**; they would knock on people's doors, sing their souling song and beg for soul cakes – little spiced buns – for the dead spirits who were thought to return at this time. These souls were remembered and prayed for on the two following days of All Saints and All Souls.

Nowadays children still go out souling at Hallowe'en in some parts of England. They hope for money for their Hallowe'en games.

Suggested accompaniments

Accompany this song with a small drum or tambour played on the beat throughout. Older children could emphasize the beat instead with the following ostinato (repeat tune) played on chime bars or xylophone:

Playing by ear

This primitive tune is based on four notes
D E F♯ G. This doesn't mean that it is
automatically easy to reproduce because the
repeated notes may confuse many children. It does
mean that the children must listen very carefully in
order to match up the notes they play with what
they sing. It also means that they must know the
tune very well before they start.

Begin with the first phrase; use the three notes
E F♯ G only and show the children how to
begin.

```
A soul, a soul, a soul cake
E  G  G F♯  F♯ G  E
```

Some children may be able to go on to play right
through the chorus which stays on these three
notes.

A Hallowe'en recipe

SPICED BUNS
200g (8 oz) self-raising flour
½ teaspoon ground cinnamon
100g (4 oz) butter or margarine
75g (30 oz) sugar
1 egg
Salt
Milk

METHOD
1 Sieve the flour, cinnamon and a pinch of salt into
   a mixing bowl.
2 Cut the fat into the flour mixture and rub in
   lightly with the tips of the fingers.
3 Add the sugar.
4 Beat up the egg and stir in. Add enough milk to
   make a stiff dough. Mix thoroughly.
5 Divide into eight portions and place on a greased
   baking tin. Brush with beaten egg, dust with
   caster sugar and bake in a moderate oven for 15 to
   20 minutes.

Hallowe'en

Music by John Wood, words by Harry Behn

Mysteriously

RECORDERS/TUNED PERCUSSION

1 To - night is the night when dead leaves fly, Like witch - es on switch - es a-cross the sky, When elf and sprite flit through the night, On a moon - y sheen, on a moon - y sheen.

2 Tonight is the night when leaves do sound,
Like gnomes in their homes far beneath the ground.
When spooks and trolls creep out of holes
Dark and mossy green, dark and mossy green.

3 Tonight is the night when pumpkins stare
Through brown sheaves and leaves almost everywhere,
When ghoul and ghost and goblin host
Dance around their queen, for it's Hallowe'en!

This song is more suitable for older children. It should be sung smoothly, quietly and very distinctly to get a feeling of mystery.

The accompaniment can provide two different tone qualities if different instruments are used for the crotchets (black notes) and the minims (open notes):
Crotchets (the introduction, middle and end phrases)
Use a recorder or xylophone for these.
Minims (two groups of four bars each)
Use chime bars, metallophone or glockenspiel for these.

Suggested percussion

Use the rhythm

(words: Through the night)

Select different short-sounding instruments for each verse:
Verse 1   claves
Verse 2   tambour – played quietly with a padded beater
Verse 3   tambourine – quietly first two lines, gaily last two lines

Playing by ear

This song is based on the following pattern of notes:
  D   E   F   G   A   Bb   C′   D′
Let the children play up and down on any tuned instrument to get used to the sound of this particular pattern. The tune is made up of a series of 'stepping' patterns. Encourage the children to listen to the way the tune moves as they sing it. Sing or hum through while you draw the shape in the air.

Provide a simple work card for the first line:

> Tonight is the night when dead leaves fly
> A D   E E F   G   A   Bb   A

Related activities

The song provides a useful framework for older children to compose their own Hallowe'en poem about what they do at this time of year.

Tonight is the night ....
When (or *like* or *as*, etc).................................
When ....
.... (repeat)...........................

The children can draw inspiration for spooky drawings or paintings from the words of the song.

Hansel and Gretel

Laurence Swinyard

Fairly slowly

mp dreamily

1 Han - sel and Gre - tel were lost in the

wood, *p* Soon it grew dark and they had - n't a - ny food. *mf* They

came up - on a house made of gin - ger - bread and spice, They

won-dered who could live in a lit - tle house so nice, *p* They won-dered who could

live in a lit - tle house so nice. *D.C.* Last time *p*

cymbal; 'shiver'

2 Standing in the doorway a wicked witch they spied,
  She *seized* the poor children and *pulled* them both inside;
  She gave a *wicked laugh* and she *rubbed her hands with glee*,
  'I'll bake you in the oven and have you for my tea,
  I'll bake you in the oven and have you for my tea.'

Suggested percussion

 cymbal 'shiver'

cymbal strikes

 a cackle then sand blocks

44

3 Close up to the oven the old witch stood,
  They *pushed* her inside and then left her there for good.
  The witch was burnt to cinders, on that you may depend,
  But Hansel and Gretel ran home and that's the end,
  But Hansel and Gretel ran home and that's the end.

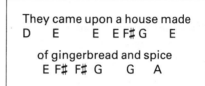

cymbal 'shiver'

cymbal strike

shakers

clappers

triangle

This simple little song outlines very clearly the well known fairy tale. It should be sung slowly in the style of a ballad. This pace is also suitable for dramatizing the song.

The *suggested percussion* is intended to underline the narrative and to accompany any mime or movement you and the children arrange. Discuss with the children what sound effects *they* would choose.

Optional accompaniment

Xylophone (starting after the introduction)
lines 1 and 2

line 3

lines 4 and 5

Playing by ear

This is a good song to illustrate shape and repetition in music. The first, second and fourth lines are based on the same tune; extra syllables are only repeat notes within the basic tune. Thus the overall shape of the song is A A B A A.

When the children can play the first line they have, in effect, learnt four fifths of the song. Start off with a simple work card for the first line:

```
Hansel and Gretel were lost in the wood
A  F♯  G  A   F♯ D      E  E  F♯  D
```

The third line uses the same five notes but in a different order:

```
They came upon a house made
D    E      E  E F♯ G    E

of gingerbread and spice
E F♯ F♯  G      G   A
```

Even if you do not introduce playing by ear, it is still a good idea to ask the children to *listen* to the song carefully to see if they can recognize the repeats of the first tune.

Related activities

Make a Hansel and Gretel house
There are ideas for a small house in *Witches and Wizards* (Macdonald). These include cardboard tubes or toilet rolls painted, stood on end and topped with a colourful painted roof made from the lumpy halves of egg boxes. For a bigger one use a cardboard carton, make a roof from card and give the children a box of suitable scraps like paper doilies, sweet papers, tissue paper, cotton wool, clean milk bottle tops, buttons and silver paper.

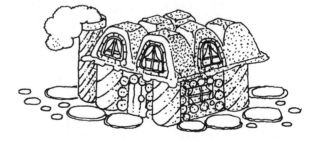

Tell the story
Illustrate, if you can, with a few taped excerpts from Humperdinck's opera *Hansel and Gretel*. A very useful book to refer to is *Heroes and Heroines in Music* by Wendy-Ann Ensor (O.U.P.). There is a good story outline, some notes about the music and an accompanying cassette which contains short selections for beginner listeners. The following are

some of the best known songs from the opera which
the children could sing:

The dance duet from Act 1, Scene 1

Gretel

1. Bro - ther, come and dance with me, Both my hands I of - fer thee,

Right foot first, left foot then, Round a - bout and back a - gain.

Hansel says he doesn't know how to dance and asks
Gretel to teach him. They sing the next verse
together, Gretel first, then Hansel.

2 With your feet you tap, tap, tap,
With your hands you clap, clap, clap,
Right foot first, left foot then,
Round about and back again.

The evening prayer from Act II, Scene II
The children, lost in the forest and very tired, sing
this prayer to comfort themselves as they rest under
a tree.

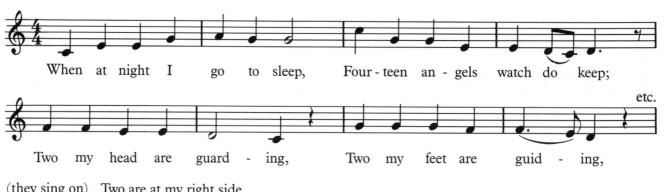

When at night I go to sleep, Four - teen an - gels watch do keep;

etc.

Two my head are guard - ing, Two my feet are guid - ing,

(they sing on) Two are at my right side,
Two are at my left side,
Two who o'er me hover,
Two above to cover,
Two to me are given
To guide my steps to heaven!

The riddle from Act II, Scene I
The children are lost in the wood. Gretel notices
some mushrooms; the song that she sings about
them is in the form of a riddle. It is often sung by
children as such.

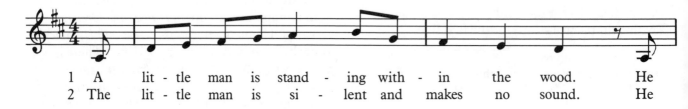

1 A lit - tle man is stand - ing with - in the wood. He
2 The lit - tle man is si - lent and makes no sound. He

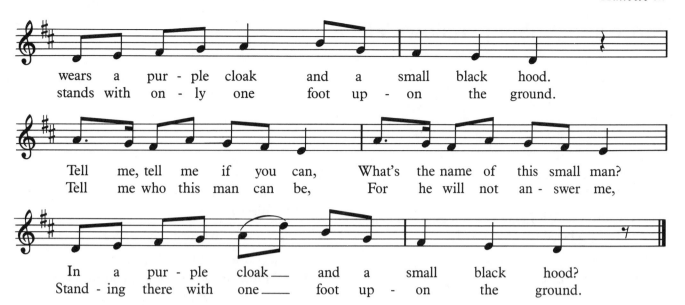

wears a pur - ple cloak and a small black hood.
stands with on - ly one foot up - on the ground.

Tell me, tell me if you can, What's the name of this small man?
Tell me who this man can be, For he will not an - swer me,

In a pur - ple cloak __ and a small black hood?
Stand - ing there with one __ foot up - on the ground.

The witch's spell from Act III, Scene II

The witch casts a spell on the children as they start
to run away. The music is dramatic whether sung in
German or English.

Hocus pocus, witch's spell!
Move, and the river will get you!
Neither forward nor backward,
I fix you with my evil eye;
Head, be rigid on the neck!

Hocus pocus, now comes Jocus!
Children, watch the magic button!
Eyes, stare straight ahead!
Now into the cage, my chap!
Hocus pocus, bonus jocus,
Malus locus, hocus pocus!

The witch's spell is broken from Act III, Scene IV

Once the witch is dead, all the children who have
been turned into gingerbread by her resume their
human forms and are completely freed by Hansel
with the aid of the witch's wand.

There are a number of good recordings of this
opera. There is only one in English – made by the
English National Opera Group (EMI SKDW 3023).

The __ spell is __ broke and __ we __ are __ free, We'll

sing and we'll dance and we'll shout __ for __ glee! Come __

child __ ren __ all, and __ form __ a __ ring, Join __

hands to - ge - ther while __ we __ sing. While __ we __ sing.

More songs about Hallowe'en

'There was an old witch'
from *Sing-a-Song Two* (Nelson)

This favourite song is full of references to sounds; percussion can be added accordingly:

> 'Swish,' goes the broomstick,
> 'Meow,' goes the cat,
> 'Plop,' goes the hop-toad
> Sitting on her hat.

Also from this collection are 'Skin and bones', a traditional ghost song from America and 'Meg and Mog', one of Helen Nicoll's stories. This has suggestions for sound effects to accompany the story.

'Hallowe'en is coming'
'Witch song' from *Sing-a-Song One* (Nelson)

Both songs are suitable for younger children. 'Hallowe'en is coming' has an interesting change of rhythm and some really spooky words. The witch song is simple and descriptive; good for the children's drawings and paintings.

'Gobbolino, the witch's cat'
by G.C. Weston from *Apusskidu* (A. & C. Black)

If you are concentrating on witches and their cats this story song is a useful one to introduce. Sing the song to the children first and they can join in the chorus:

> 'Who'll give a home to a kitten?
> Who'll give a home to a cat?
> Gobbolino you may call me;
> I want just a fire and a mat.'

'Hallowe'en's coming'
From *Singing Fun* by Lucille Wood and Louise Scott (Harrap)

This song is suitable for younger children. It is based on five notes only and contains some simple phrases that can be played on chimes or recorders.

'Spooky'
by H.C. and V.P. Mitchell from *Harlequin* (A. & C. Black)

The last verse is 'in case of nightmares!':

> Witches! Witches! Big and black,
> The Hallowe'en witches won't come back.
> Fly away! Fly away! Don't come back.
> The Hallowe'en witches won't come back.
> (younger children)

'We're witches of Hallowe'en'
from *Knock at the door* by Jan Betts (Ward Lock Educational)

One from a group of witch songs and poems for younger children.

'Jackie Jack o' Lantern'
from *The Magic of Music Book 1* (Ginn & Co)

This is the title of a group of songs connected by a story. It can be treated as an entire unit or the songs can be sung separately. It is based on a Hallowe'en party to which the children come wearing masks. It comprises:

> 'Hurray for Hallowe'en!' about Hallowe'en
> 'Are you ready?' about going to the party
> 'Who's a-knocking?' to welcome Jack-o'-lantern
> 'Hallowe'en Parade' a ghosts' and goblins' march
> 'See me in my false face' a mask song
> 'High and Low' a witch's song
> 'Hurrah for Hallowe'en!' a repeat

Suitable for younger children.

A Festival for Autumn
by Anne Mendoza (Novello)

This selection includes a witches' chant and a witches' song and dance. The complete group of ten items is intended 'for dramatic presentation or concert performance'. It is arranged for voices, descant recorders, guitar, cello and tuned and untuned percussion. It is more suitable for older children.

Poems

In the dark, dark wood, there was
a dark, dark house,
And in that dark, dark house, there was
a dark, dark room,
And in that dark, dark room, there was
a dark, dark cupboard,
And in that dark, dark cupboard, there was
a dark, dark shelf,
And on that dark, dark shelf, there was
a dark, dark box,
And in that dark, dark box, there was a
GHOST!

Anon

Wild witches' ball

late last night at wildwitchhall
we witches held our wild witch ball.
in every size and shape and weight
we witches came to celebrate.

ten tall crones with moans and groans
battled in barrels with bats and bones.
nine queer dears with pointed ears
dangled and swang from the chandeliers.

witches eight with mangy tresses
danced with seven sorceresses.
witches six in shaggy rags
played toss and tag with five old hags.

four fat bags took healthy bites
from parts of three unsightly frights.
two fierce furies dug a ditch
and tumbled in on lumpy witch.

there were witches squeezed in every nook
whichever where you cared to look.
how many witches can you see
at our annual wildwitch witches' spree?

Jack Prelutsky

Witch, Witch

'Witch, witch, where do you fly?' . . .
'Under the clouds and over the sky.'

'Witch, witch, what do you eat?' . . .
'Little black apples from Hurricane Street.'

'Witch, witch, what do you drink?' . . .
'Vinegar, blacking and good red ink.'

'Witch, witch, where do you sleep?' . . .
'Up in the clouds where pillows are cheap.'

Rose Fyleman

Witch goes shopping

Witch rides off
Upon her broom
Finds a space
To park it.
Takes a shiny shopping cart
Into the supermarket.
Smacks her lips and reads
The list of things she needs:
  'Six bats' wings
  Worms in brine
  Ears of toads
  Eight or nine.
  Slugs and bugs
  Snake skins dried
  Buzzard innards
  Pickled, fried.'
Witch takes herself
From shelf to shelf
Cackling all the while.
Up and down and up and down and
In and out each aisle.
Out comes cans and cartons
Tumbling to the floor.
'This,' says Witch, now all a-twitch
'Is a crazy store.
I CAN'T FIND A SINGLE THING
I AM LOOKING FOR!'

Lilian Moore

Old Moll

The moon is up,

    The night owls scritch

Who's that croaking?

    The frog in the ditch.

Who's that howling?

    The old hound bitch.

My neck tingles,

    My elbows itch

My hair rises,

    My eyelids twitch.

What's in that pot

    So rare and rich?

Who's that crouching

    In a cloak like pitch?

Hush! that's Old Moll –

    They say she's a

Most ree-markable old party.

        Leonard Clark

An obvious basis for phonic work on the sound 'itch'.

Sound picture

Try to build up an atmospheric night-time picture, and add and subtract, in any order, the sounds highlighted in this poem finishing with the sounds of Old Moll and her cooking.

    The main night-time group could include *a cymbal played quietly with a padded beater*, some windy *vocal* sounds, rustling sounds from dried leaves e.g. *shakers, or random chime bar notes* representing the moon and stars. This group could work out a pattern of sound that could go on all the

Suggested sounds

 quiet triangle

vocal *oo-oo-oo*

vocal or rasp

vocal

 trilled triangle

 scraped drum/tambourine

 cymbal

 shaker

 wobble on the xylophone (bubbling)

 cymbal – strike quietly with padded beater

child slinks by dressed as a witch – everyone cackles

time. The other sounds made by individual children (or small groups) can then play at intervals against the background of the main group. Finally bring in the sounds of Old Moll – cooking and cackles. The sound picture could end with a *cymbal 'shiver'*, or the night-time sounds could stop one by one leaving just the quiet notes of the moon and stars as an ending.

More poems

Witch Poems }   edited by Daisy Wallace
Ghost Poems }   (Pepper Press)
'Hallowe'en' by Eleanor Farjeon } *Time's Delights*
'The hag' by Robert Herrick } (Beaver Books)

'Moths and moonshine' by James Reeves
The Young Puffing Book of Verse

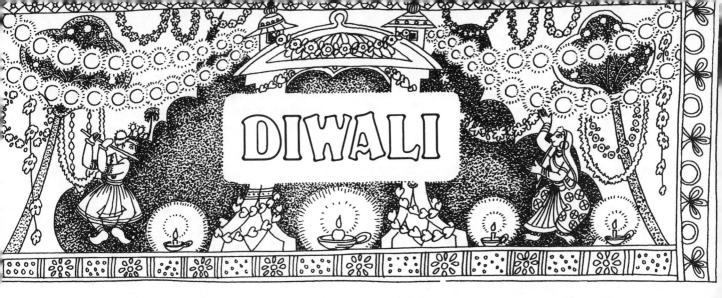

Background information

Diwali (also spelt Divali) is the Indian festival of lights. It is celebrated by Hindus and occurs during the month of October or November. The date varies. It celebrates the victory of Rama over the demon king Ravana and his triumphant return to Ayodhaya after 14 years' exile. Diwali is also regarded as the beginning of a new year for it is the time of the sowing of the winter rice crop.

The story of Rama and Sita comes from an epic poem written in Sanskrit by the sage or holy man Valmiki about 3,000 years ago. This is called the **Ramayana** and different versions of it are popular in different parts of India although the plot remains the same.

Rama is the example of obedience and dutifulness; he obeyed his father, gave up his claim to the throne and never faltered in his efforts to find Sita, his wife, when she was captured by the demon king Ravana. In a deeper context he is held to be one of the incarnations of Vishnu, the Lord and Preserver of Mankind, who has often taken the form of a man or a creature, and lived among men on at least eight occasions.

The beautiful and gentle Sita has been worshipped as the Divine Mother. She personifies truth, while Ravana stands for falsehood and Rama the fighter for truth. For Hindus Rama and Sita represent the ideal man and woman.

The time of Diwali is a very happy one. Everyone decorates their home with lights or little lamps, called divas, the streets are hung with garlands of flowers and are full of lights as they were for Rama's homecoming. People wear their best clothes or buy new ones, children are given presents and new year greetings are exchanged through visits or Diwali cards. Everywhere is clean and shiny for Hindus believe in the cleanliness of body, mind and home.

Diwali can be celebrated in schools in this country through activities stemming from the story of Rama and Sita. Children can write all or parts of the story and paint or draw their illustrations. A class story book could be assembled from the children's efforts. Classrooms could be decorated and Diwali cards designed. The story of Rama and Sita could be dramatized as suggested in the latter part of this section, or a dance drama could be presented.

Art and craft

Diwali lamps

Any craft work involving a candle with a naked flame is not recommended unless used as a 'diva' or little light under the strictest supervision.

The children could use plasticine or clay to make little cup-like dishes and shape with a handle. Very small night lights will then complete the Diwali lamp.

Alternatively, small picnic plates or saucers, highly decorated, and holding a toilet roll candle with a sparkly paper flame will give the impression of lighted lamps.

Hanging garlands (Pandals)

These are traditional for many festivities. Improvise your own design for flowers made from coloured tissue paper and hang them, using a light rod or twig or small hoop.

The children's paper flowers could also be fixed on to twigs held in a small flower pot by plasticine.

Decorative designs (Rangoli)

Provide a template, pencil in the main design and let the children improvise their own patterns round the edge. Arrange the children's finished designs on a large sheet or turn into a pattern frieze.

A foil milk top makes a good centre

Build up the lotus flower with cut out petals

The children could also look at Indian designs on cards and patterns on saris, etc.

Traditionally floor patterns are frequently used for decoration in the Indian home during Diwali and are executed with either a paste of rice flour, paint and water, or with dry powders. Parents might be able to help and advise with patterns and techniques.

The following outlines can be used as centre designs for picnic plates or table mats. They can also be turned into (highly decorated) standing models made out of stiff paper or card. Finish plates and models with a coat of varnish.

supporting flap or bottom half of second cut-out used to back the first

Festival food

Barphi

Sweetmeats are favourite festival foods. The following is a simplified version of *barphi* (or *barfi*), little sweets made from a milk base:

150g (6 oz) sugar   1 teacup
100ml water   ½ teacup
200g (8 oz) milk powder   2 teacups

Optional decorations
1 teaspoon crushed cardamom seeds
12 pistachio nuts finely sliced
Edible silver leaf or balls

METHOD
1 Boil the sugar and water together fairly quickly for six or seven minutes until the mixture begins to thicken. This will need special arrangements because of the danger of scalding water.

2 Add the milk powder gradually. The mixture should become fairly firm but soft and pliable. The amount of powder will depend upon the degree of boiling down of the sugar and water, so all the powder may not be needed. Alternatively a little more can be added if the mixture is not firm enough.

3 Turn the mixture into a well-greased shallow baking pan or enamel plate. Pat and spread with the palms of hands and cut into squares or other shapes. The barphi is ready to eat when it becomes firm.

Decorations are optional but will provide an opportunity for the children to handle and arrange them and for them to learn about the seeds and nuts. Makes about 20 pieces.

To make *coconut barphi* add about two tablespoons of dessicated coconut to the mixture and decorate with more coconut, chopped nuts and cherries. There are more variations using different flavours and decorations, all based on the plain mixture.

Samosas are popular tea-time savouries and will most certainly feature among festival foods. They are little triangular pastries stuffed with potato and peas or meat, rather like a small Cornish pasty. Traditionally the pastry is made with plain flour, warm milk, salt and butter-fat. The latter is prepared from cooked and strained butter. The filled cases are then deep fried and served hot with mint or tamarind chutney at teatime.

Indian music and musical instruments

A **raga** is a group of notes rather like our scale; there are 250 ragas in Indian music each creating special sounds for special moods. There are, for instance, different ragas for the different times of the day. Melodies are based on specific ragas like the one used in 'The story of Diwali in song'.

Indian music nearly always has a background **drone**, usually based on the first and fifth notes of the raga and having a steady rhythm. Within the basic rhythmic cycle or **tala** many complicated rhythms can be added as decorative patterns. This will be apparent, in a simplified form, if the suggested accompaniments are added to the Diwali song.

Improvisation is an important element in Indian music. The children can complement the sound of the songs in this section by making their own improvisations as suggested in the song notes.

The **sitar** is the best known melodic instrument. It has seven strings passing over a bridge and twelve 'sympathetic' strings lying beneath the main playing strings. The end of the sitar is shaped like a gourd; this amplifies the sounds. The strings are plucked with a plectrum.

The **sarangi**, also a melody instrument, is the equivalent of the violin; smaller than the sitar it has three or four bowed strings and some 'sympathetic' ones. A **flute** is often included in the melody players.

The **tambura** plays the drone. It has only four strings and is similar in shape to the sitar.

The **tabla** provides the percussion element. It consists of two drums, one made of copper and one made of wood. There is also a folk double drum rather like a pair of bongo drums joined together.

Leela Floyd's book and cassette on *Indian Music* in the *Oxford Topics in Music* series (O.U.P.) will provide more details and listening examples.

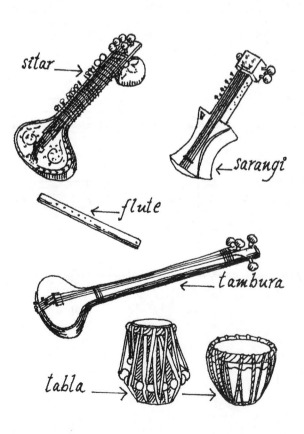

sitar →   ← sarangi   ← flute   ← tambura   tabla →

The story of Diwali in song

Punitha Perinparaja

Clearly and with a steady rhythm

INTRODUCTION

Dee - pa - va - li _____ Dee - pa - va - - li _____ Dee - pa - va - li _____

CHORUS

Je - ya, Je - ya, Ra - ma, _____ Je - ya, Je - ya, Si - ta, _____

Dee - pa - va - li _____ Dee - pa - va - li _____

Fine

Dee - pa - va - li _____

VERSE 1

Ra - ma and Si - ta _____ lived in the fo - rest,

Wi - cked king Ra - va - na cap - tured Si - ta, _____

Ra - ma de - clared war. _____

Em
Ha-nu-man's ar-my helped him._____ Return to CHORUS

C   G   Em   G   C
De-mon king was slain,   Si - ta is back a - gain.

VERSE 2

G   C
Dark - ness is end - ed,_____ gone the sad days,_____

C
Come light the lamps and   let it spread its rays._____

C
Ra - ma is the king._____

Em
Peo - ple_____ of A - yo-dya__ greet him._____

C   G   C Return to CHORUS
Flow - ers we bring,   let's dance_ and __ sing._____

This lovely song outlines in two verses part of the story of Rama and Sita. It can be accompanied with simple percussion, movement and mime. It is set to a South Indian Adi-Tala with a beat of eight counts but North Indian Teental can be used.

Teaching suggestions

Some of the decorations sung by the singer on the cassette accompanying this book have been left out in the music here to clarify the basic structure of the melody. So when you have introduced the song let the children listen to the cassette several times to get the feel and basic pulse of the music. It will not be long before they will be able to join in with the chorus 'Jeya, Jeya, Rama . . .' and to copy some of the decorations on the word 'Deepavali'. These decorations which are typical of Indian singing are, in fact, improvisations and will vary with each singer, but the basic melody remains.

As the song begins to take shape add selected percussion from the following suggestions. A drum or tambour is easy to start with and bells and tambourine on the chorus. The other suggestions can be used according to the abilities of your group and the strength of the singers.

Diwali

Introduction

recorder and/or glockenspiel

Play once through as an instrumental introduction.

The song (beginning with the chorus)

recorder and/or glockenspiel

piano   etc.

right hand - melody

left hand - drone

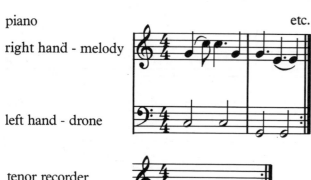

tenor recorder

descant recorder

bass xylophone

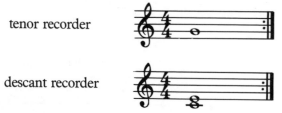

Indian bells
(chorus)

drum (muffled first
beat throughout)

tambourine
(chorus)

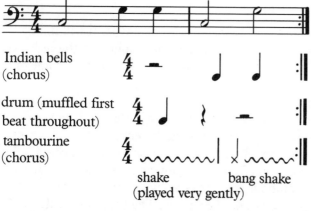

shake   bang shake
(played very gently)

suspended cymbal
(dying away naturally)   Rama is the king

Guitar note It is not usual to harmonize Indian tunes. However, guitar chords have been incorporated in the song notes as they may be useful to help the teaching of the song and to keep the rhythm going. It is a good idea to dispense with the guitar as soon as the song is established. This is the time to introduce any accompaniments that are going to be used as they should not be played at the same time as the guitar.

Movement

Teach this movement to the whole class, then choose a small group to accompany the song.

Step to accompany the introduction and chorus is basically a rhythmic walk, it becomes: *step, step, step, bend; step, step, step, bend;* and so on. The bend is just a slow knee bend as the third step is taken. Thus the feet used are:
left, right, left – bend; right, left, right – bend; and so on.
Movement for 'Jeya, Jeya, Rama, Jeya, Jeya, Sita': group into a circle joining hands and continue the basic step twice to the left then twice to the right, once into the middle, once out and turn round on the spot.

Thus the final shape could be:
Deepavali, Deepavali, Deepavali:
Children enter in a line doing the basic step, then form into a circle.
Jeya, Jeya, Rama,
Jeya, Jeya, Sita,
Basic step to the left.
Jeya, Jeya, Rama,
Jeya, Jeya, Sita,
Basic step to the right.
Deepavali, Deepavali, Deepavali.
Basic step into the middle.
Basic step out again and turn round on the spot.

Mime

Choose three children to represent Rama, Sita and the wicked king Ravana and let them mime all the actions as Verse 1 is sung. The movements should be dignified. Ravana is slain by a bow from Rama's arrow.

Rama and Sita can slowly approach the dancing circle during the next chorus. Verse 2 can be mimed by the dancing group while Rama and Sita stand regally or sit on 'thrones'. Everyone exits in procession to the last chorus all doing the basic step.

Costume

Girls can wear saris or brightly coloured dresses with a sash draped over one shoulder, and flower(s) in their hair. Sita should wear a really bright and beautiful sari; she can also wear a coloured band in her hair.

Boys can wear coloured shirts, coloured trousers, or ordinary trousers with a bright sash draped across one shoulder. Rama and Ravana can wear turban-like crowns.

Musical activities

This song is based on a raga which, as written, uses only the following notes: C D E G B C'. Put out the chime bars in this order in the music corner so that the children can play up and down to get used to the sound of this arrangement of notes. Felt beaters will make the sound more tolerable in the classroom.

Encourage the children to base their playing on a particular rhythm:

OR

They can also use a particular sequence of notes to play up and down:

The player can, if he wishes, change the rhythm for the descending passage. The suggestion above echoes the basic rhythm of this Diwali song. Two beaters will make it easier to play. Keep this as a challenge for the more rhythmically able child! Let the others keep a steady beat and concentrate on going up and coming down in sequence.

A second child can now accompany with a 'drone' which can be one or two notes chosen from the group being used:

The 'drone' player will accompany the raga picking up the rhythm of that player. An older or more experienced child might improvise a little tune which could also be accompanied by a suitable drone.

Diwali

Subbash Mukker

Happily

1 Jhi - ll mi - ll jhi - ll mi - ll deep_____ ja - la - o

aa - j Di - wa - li a - yee_____

CHORUS 1 (first time only)

Na - cho __ ga - o __ khu-shi __ ma - na - o __ aa - j Di - wa - li

a - yee_____ aa - j Di - wa - li __ a - yee._____

CHORUS 2 (after Verse 2–7)

Jhi - ll mi - ll jhi - ll mi - ll deep ___ ja - la - o ___ aa - j Di - wa - li __

a - yee_____ aa - j Di - wa - li __ a - yee

2 I am going to buy some nice new toys
And you will get some today.

CHORUS

3 Fireworks will be let off this evening
It is Diwali today.

CHORUS

4 I am going to put on my nice new clothes,
It is Diwali today.

CHORUS

5 I am going to eat some coloured sweetmeats,
It is Diwali today.

CHORUS

6 Look at all the decorations, look at the candles,
It is Diwali today.

CHORUS

7 I am going to worship with my hands joined together,
Because Lakshmi has come.
(Lakshmi is the Goddess of Wealth)

CHORUS

Translation

Chorus 1

Nacho gao khushi manao aaj Diwali means 'laugh and be merry because it is Diwali today.'

Chorus 2

Jhill mill jhill deep jalao aaj Diwali means 'light the lamps because it is Diwali today.'

Pronunciation

Jhill mill – jil-le mil-le

aaj – aa-je

Lakshmi is the Goddess of Wealth

Finish with the introductory verse and chorus as written.

Mrs Mukker's song sounds beautiful sung in the original language, so it is suggested that the children sing the introduction, chorus and last verse in Hindi. Teach this phonetically as written.

When singing this song try to underline the rhythmic element. This will help the children especially with the long musical ending of 'ayee . . .'. The English words do fit the rhythm of the first four bars of the song but not always with the musical accents that we are used to. It is a good idea therefore to give yourself plenty of practice fitting in the words to the tune before you sing with the children.

Mrs Mukker suggests that her song can also be sung to the tune of 'Train is a-coming' as follows:

1 Di wa - li is com - ing,__ Oh__ yes! Di wa -li is com - ing,__ Oh__ yes!

Di wa - li is com - ing, Di-wa -li is com - ing, Di-wa -li is com - ing, Oh__ yes!

2 Laugh and be merry, merry . . .

3 I am going to buy some new toys . . .

4 Sparkling fireworks will crackle . . .

5 I am going to wear my new clothes . . .

6 I am going to eat lots of sweetmeats . . .

7 I am going to worship Lakshmi . . .

8 Lights on the candles are dancing . . .

9 Everyone is happy, happy . . .

Encourage the children to work out how they will add the percussion. It need not be the same for each verse; it will depend upon the age and musical background of the children. Here are some suggestions:

The children could go on to make up some of their own verses about Rama and Sita.

Suggested percussion

	tambourine
	shakers
	bells
	shakers
	sand blocks
	quiet singing
	triangle
	all percussion

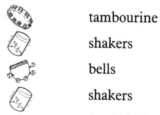

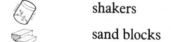

tambourine

shakers — play gently throughout

bells

sand blocks — play throughout

triangle

Rama, the king of kings   Raghupati Raghava Raja Ram

In the style of a chant   Traditional Indian religious chant adapted and arranged by Punitha Perinparaja

CHORUS

Ra-ma is the great-est __ king of kings, _____ Ra-ma the pur-est, Si - ta Ram.
Rag-hu pat-i Ra-ga-va Ra - ja Ram_____ Pat-hi-i-ta pa-va-na Si - ta Ram.

VERSE

1. Si - ta Ram,_____ Si - ta Ram, Prai-ses we sing to __ Si - ta Ram.
Si - ta Ram,_____ Si - ta Ram, Ba - ju pya - re ma-ne _ Si - ta Ram.

VARIATION

Ra-ma is the great - est _ king of kings, _____ Ra - ma the pur-est, Si - ta Ram.
Rag-hu pat-i Ra-ga-va Ra - ja Ram, _____ Pat-hi-i-ta pa-va-na Si - ta Ram.

SUGGESTED ENDING

Ra - ma Ra - ma, Ra - ma Ra - ma, Ra - ma Ra - ma _ Ram.

Ra - ma Si - ta, Ra - ma Si - ta, Ra - ma Si - ta Ram.

2 Eeshvar, Allah are the names of God,
   Grant us the wisdom that comes from the Lord.
   Eeshvar, Allah, Tere, nam,
   Sab ko sunmati de Bagvan.

Note Because the English version does not convey the precise meaning of the Hindi, a meaning as close as possible to this highly philosophical song has been attempted:
Chorus
'Raghu pati Raghava Raja Ram' are the many names of Rama who is the leader of the Raghu dynasty,
Rama whose purity has transcended the corrupt world, Sita Ram.
Verse 1
Sita Ram, Sita Ram
Repeat in your hearts the names of Sita and Ram.
Verse 2
Eeshvar, Allah are the names of God,
Grant us the wisdom that comes from the Lord.

This religious chant is called a **Bhajan**. It is typical of the many religious chants sung in India and is one of the most popular among Hindus. It was said to be a favourite of Mahatma Gandhi who adapted the wording so that it could incorporate the various religions practised in India.

Raghupati Raghava Raja Ram is an invocation to God and can be sung at all times, but because of its reference to Rama and Sita it is particularly relevant to the festival of Diwali. It is included here for its musical value as well, for it represents a simple melodic style that is sung by ordinary people in India.

A leader usually sings each part first and this is repeated by the rest of the congregation or group. Each section can be sung more than once or twice and the order in which the sections are sung can vary. When the song is well known, teachers might like to divide the children into, say, two groups and build up their own arrangement.

More songs from India

'Diwali'

from *Tinder-box* (A. & C. Black)

This festival song has words in English and Gujerati which describe traditional activities at this time of year.

Diwas lighted in every house,
Rangoli patterns in every house.
Decorations on every door,
Tiny stars are shining bright.

Also by Niru Desai is the song 'Majapada' ('Let's all be happy') with words in both languages, and a finger play song about hands from Punitha Perinparaja with additional words in Tamil.

'Song of the Delhi Tongawallah'

from *Sing-a-Song Two* (Nelson)

The Tongawallah is a pony-cart driver. This song can be sung with sound effects from yoghurt pots or coconut shells and jingles. This collection has a song and story about some travelling musicians and a rich Raja – Bhindoo, Bhadoo, Bhidoo – and an amusing song about Nellie the Elephant who went to Bombay. Both these melodies are western.

Recorded music

Raga Rang: a tapestry of Indian classical instrumental music EMI ECSD 2773 (stereo)
Any of the tracks from this record, especially *Bhatiyali* (Side 1, Track 2) with flute and bells would be suitable. This record is typical of many available from the EMI catalogue which would provide suitable music to accompany the Diwali play.

The story of Diwali

Once upon a time, many, many years ago in the land of India, there was a good king who ruled over the kingdom of Ayodhaya. He had three wives who were all queens, for in those days kings were allowed to have more than one wife. He also had four sons, but his favourite was Rama, the eldest.

As time went on Rama's father found that he was getting too old and tired to rule; he decided to ask his son Rama to be king in his place. His other sons all agreed that Rama was the right one to rule but one of their mothers was envious because she wanted her son Prince Bharata to be king. She remembered that the old king had promised her two boons (or wishes) a long time ago, so she decided to claim them straight away. She asked for her son Bharata to be made king and for Rama to be banished to the forest for 14 years. The king was very sad but could not go back on his promise. Rama knew that he should support his father and left willingly to go and live in the forest. Beautiful Sita, his wife, and his best loved brother, Lakshmana, went with him.

The old king was heartbroken and died soon afterwards. Bharata refused to be king and went into the forest to ask his brother to come back. But Rama would not break his promise to stay in the forest for 14 years, so Bharata asked for Rama's golden sandals to take back and put on the throne as a sign that he would look after the country until Rama, the true king, returned.

Rama, Sita and Lakshmana lived happily in the forest for ten years. They built a fine hut of bamboo and made friends with all the forest animals.

Now there were also many wicked demons who lived in India at this time. One of the fiercest called Ravana had ten arms and ten heads. He hated Rama and decided to capture Sita and take her back to the island of Lanka where he lived. He had to make sure that Sita was by herself for Rama would most certainly kill him. So he changed one of his demon followers into a beautiful golden deer. When Sita saw the lovely little animal she asked Rama to catch it, for it went bounding off into the forest. Rama wanted to please Sita; but before he left he told his brother Lakshmana to stay to protect her.

Then the demon tricked Sita. He imitated Rama's voice calling to Lakshmana for help. Sita was frightened that Rama might be hurt and ordered Lakshmana to go. Faithful Lakshmana drew a magic circle around the hut to protect Sita while he was gone. Then Ravana, disguised as a poor beggar, came to Sita begging for food and drink. He persuaded her to step outside the magic circle so that he could capture her and carry her off in his flying chariot. Poor Sita was helpless. She shouted and struggled as she was tied up and flown away to Ravana's palace. When she refused to marry him Ravana was furious. He kept her in the palace gardens where she lived as a prisoner.

When Rama and his brother returned to their hut they found it empty. Sita had disappeared. Heartbroken, they realized they had been tricked and started a long search for their beloved Sita. They were helped by all the monkeys who went north, south, east and west to look for her. One of them met an old vulture who was able to tell them where Sita was – a long, long, way away on the island of Lanka. The king of the monkeys called Hanuman could fly and went immediately to find where Sita was and how Rama could get her back. He returned to Rama and together they planned a great battle. They built a huge bridge of rocks so that they could all get across to the island. Ravana was ready for them with his mighty army. There was a great battle between Ravana and his demons and Rama, Hanuman and the monkeys which lasted ten days. In the end Rama challenged Ravana, but Ravana was so strong that Rama's arrows didn't hurt him. Then the gods lent Rama a special bow and with this he shot the final arrow that killed Ravana. The battle was won.

Sita was overjoyed when Hanuman told her that Ravana was dead. She was free to be with Rama again. Together with Lakshmana, Hanuman and all the monkeys they returned to the kingdom of Ayodhaya, for the banishment was now over.

Bharata welcomed his brother Rama back as the rightful king and ordered a public holiday for the people to celebrate. All the buildings were decorated; flags and garlands of flowers were hung everywhere and thousands of small lamps were lit throughout the city to guide King Rama back home to his palace. Rama and Sita were crowned king and queen and together they ruled the kingdom of Ayodhaya wisely and well for many years.

Every year Hindus celebrate the victory of Rama over the evil demon Ravana and they remember the way the people of Ayodhaya lighted their city to welcome Rama and Sita and to guide them back. Here are some suggestions for dramatization:

Characters
The king of Ayodhaya
Queen Kaikeyi, the mother of Bharata
Prince Rama
Prince Lakshmana
Prince Shatrughna   } sons of the king
Prince Bharata
Princess Sita
Ravana the wicked demon
The golden deer, another demon in disguise
Hanuman, king of the monkeys
Monkeys
Demons
Animals in the forest: fawns, peacocks, monkeys
Courtiers
Messenger

Set the scene by playing some recorded Indian music.

Scene 1

A *slow quiet drum* provides an entry for the old king followed by some members of his court. He tells them that he is too old to rule and must choose his successor. A messenger fetches the four sons who kneel before the king. The latter says he wishes Rama to be king. All the sons agree. Rama stands up and promises to be as good a ruler as his father. (*Exit to a slow quiet drum beat.*)

Scene 2

Queen Kaikeyi enters (*quiet bells*). She tells everyone she has heard about the king's plans for Rama; but she has a son who she thinks ought to be king. She has a plan to make her son king. The king enters slowly (*drum beat*). The queen asks for her two boons. The king sadly agrees. He sits on the throne. A messenger

fetches Rama who enters (*drum beat*). The king tells Rama and Lakshmana, who has also heard the king's message, that Rama must leave at once to spend 14 years in the forest in exile. Rama agrees.

Lakshmana is furious but insists on going with Rama. Enter Sita who wonders why the king is looking so sad. They tell her. She also insists on going with Rama. They leave the king to get ready to leave. Exit the king distraught.

Scene 3

The two princes and Sita enjoy the forest, walking and playing with the animals. Enter Bharata to ask Rama to return to the kingdom as their father is now dead. Rama refuses but agrees to give Bharata his golden sandals. Exit Bharata with sandals. A *drum beat* indicates the passing of time. A golden deer frolics in to entice Sita, who persuades Rama to follow it as it runs away. Lakshmana stays with Sita until Rama's voice is heard calling for help. Lakshmana draws a circle round Sita before he goes. Enter the demon Ravana as a beggar (*cymbal shiver*). He captures Sita as she comes to help him and takes her off. Rama and Lakshmana return to find Sita has disappeared. They search everywhere. Enter the monkeys who offer to help. They agree to search north, east, south and west. All exit.

Scene 4

An old vulture is squatting on the ground. Enter a monkey searching for Sita. He asks the vulture if he has seen her. The vulture explains where he thinks Sita is. It is too far to go. Enter Hanuman, king of the monkeys, with Rama and Lakshmana. He flies off. The others settle anxiously to wait. A *quiet drum beat* indicates the passing of time. Hanuman returns with the news that he has found Sita on the island of Lanka. They plan a great battle against Ravana and march round on their journey. Coming to the sea they build a bridge across to the island. (*Do this with PE forms or stage blocks*.) Accompany the setting up with *drums* and *wood blocks* for building sounds. Everyone exits.

Scene 5

This is the battle scene between the monkeys and the demons. Keep the 'bridge' to the back of the stage. It will form a line of 'trees' for some of the

monkeys to climb on. Let the opposing groups come in slowly each side to a *slow drum beat*. They will mime a simple fight. Then Rama and Ravana enter on their respective sides while Hanuman stands up at the back. Use a *drum beat* to bring them on and a *cymbal* as they take up positions. Rama and Ravana will have bows and will mime the shooting of arrows. When Ravana finally falls, the monkeys and Rama raise their arms in victory. Hanuman fetches Sita. Exit everyone; Rama's group in happy procession one side; the demons dejectedly the other side. *Drums and bells* can accompany this exit. (*This battle scene could be omitted or covered by a narrator*.)

Scene 6

Enter a group of people of Ayodhaya with the queens and Bharata carrying lights/lamps. They group themselves to one side ready to receive Rama, Sita, Lakshmana, Hanuman and the monkey army. Rama and Sita are crowned king and queen. There can be a final procession with Rama and Sita at the head with as many lights, streamers and flowers as you wish. Use *recorded music* to bring the children on at the beginning of the scene and for the final procession. *Hand bells* can also be carried.

Suggested music

Percussion

drum – a bongo drum played with the fingers most closely resembles the Indian drum or tabla. Encourage the player to discover how many different sounds can be obtained from the head of the drum. A more experienced child could use two different-sized bongo drums to help produce suitable rhythms and effects.

cymbal – a large cymbal, especially a suspended one, will provide good dramatic background sound effects.

bells – any type of bell-like sound – finger cymbals, Indian bells, jingles but especially hand bells – will be suitable.

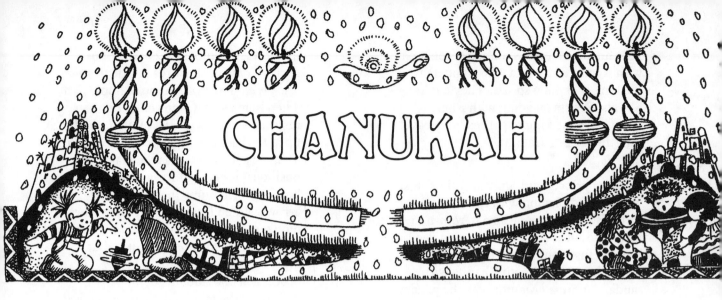

Background information

Chanukah is the Jewish festival of lights. It is an eight-day festival, usually celebrated in December and commemorates the uprising against the Syrian King Antiochus in the year 165 B.C. The victorious Maccabee family and their followers regained Jerusalem and inaugurated an eight-day dedication of the Temple. The story is told that they found only one jar of the pure oil that was needed to light the flame of thanksgiving. Although this would not last for more than one day it kept the lamp burning for the full eight days and nights until more oil could be prepared. This was regarded as a miracle by the Jews.

Today the festival of Chanukah – meaning dedication – celebrates this miracle. Every Jewish home has a **menorah**, which is an eight-branched candelabrum or special candlestick. One candle is lit and placed in the menorah every night of the holiday.

It is a happy festival with special songs and food and often presents for each night. Traditionally children are given a special toy called a **dreidel** (pronounced dray-dle). This is a many sided spinning top which seems to characterize the gaiety of the festival.

Note Chanukah has other accepted spellings: Hanukkah, Chanucah, Hannukah.

Art and craft

Simple dreidel

Decorate an 8 cm square piece of thin cardboard. Prick a small hole in the centre and insert a toothpick or pencil.

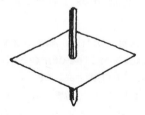

Model dreidel

Cut a shape out of thin cardboard and decorate the sides.

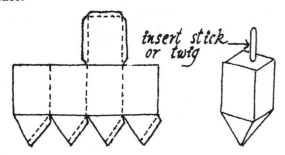

Fold the cardboard along the dotted lines and paste together to form the dreidel.

Games can be played with the dreidel by writing a letter on each of its sides. You win or lose depending upon the letter uppermost when the dreidel stops spinning. In a game with counters the following Hebrew letters are often used:

נ   Nothing happens

ג   Take all

ה   Take half

ש   Put in one counter

Mobile

Bend some coat hanger wire into the shape of a dreidel and hang some small paper dreidels, candles or other symbolic shapes.

(The game is escribed in *Craft in Action*, see *Resources* page 185.)

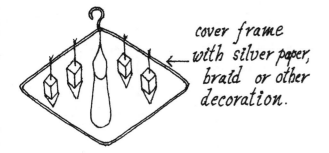

Festival food

Potato pancakes and butter biscuits are firm favourites for Chanukah.

Potato pancakes (latkes)

6 medium sized potatoes
2 eggs
50g (2 oz) self-raising flour or fine matzomeal
1 teaspoon salt; pepper
Oil for deep frying in a thick frying pan

METHOD
1 Peel and finely grate the potatoes into a bowl of cold water.
2 Leave for five minutes then strain through a muslin bag. Make sure that all excess liquid is drained off to ensure good pancakes.
3 Mix all the ingredients to a thick batter.
4 Heat the oil and drop in tablespoons of the mixture to make pancakes of about 8 cm across.
5 Fry on both sides until nicely brown.
6 Drain on kitchen paper.

The cooking in oil must be done by an adult and this recipe would be safer in the hands of a parent with a special knowledge of Jewish cooking.

Butter biscuits (kuchlich)

200g (8 oz) self-raising flour
125g (5 oz) butter or margarine
75g (3 oz) sugar
2 medium sized eggs
pinch salt
grated rind of a lemon

METHOD
1 Sieve flour with salt and rub in butter.
2 Add sugar and mix well.
3 Beat eggs until frothy and add to mixture.
4 Add lemon rind.
5 Knead and roll out to ½ cm thickness.
6 Cut into rounds or special shapes.
7 Place on greased tin and bake in moderate oven until nicely browned.

Chanukah

Traditional folk song translated by Rita Kalev

Gaily

C

Cha - nu - kah, Cha - nu - kah, What a love - ly time.
Cha - nu - kah, Cha - nu - kah, chag ya - fe kol kach.

G7

Co - loured lights all a - round Joy for eve - ry child.
Or cha - viv mi - sa - viv gil l' - ye - led rach.

Cha - nu - kah, Cha - nu - kah, Spin - ning top goes round.
Cha - nu - kah, Cha - nu - kah s' - Vi - von sov sov.

G7

Spin, spin, spin, spin, spin, spin, All a - bout the ground.
Sov, sov, sov, sov, sov, sov, ma na - im va - tov.

Singing game

In a circle:
line 1 – seven skips to the left and stop
line 2 – seven skips to the right and stop
line 3 – clap
line 4 – skip round on the spot, single or with a
partner

Suggested percussion

 tambourine
on the beat

 add shakers

Spinning top   S'Vivon

Traditional Hebrew song translated by Judith Rabin

Dance

(older children)

Form in two concentric circles, hands joined or on shoulders.

line 1 – outer circle walks to the left in time with the music while inner circle walks to the right

line 2 – circles change direction

line 3 – outer circle kneels and claps while inner circle spiral like tops in pairs or on their own

line 4 – circles change places and dance begins again

Suggested percusson

tambourine   repeat four times

Potato pancakes   L'Vivot

N. Nardi. **English** words from a translation by Judith Rabin

Playfully

1 Flour,＿ flour＿ from the sack, Oil,＿ oil＿ from the jug.
Ke - mach, ke - mach min ha - sak, She-men, she-men min ha - kad.

Cha - nu - kah is here, Fes - ti - val of cheer.
Cha - nu - kah ha - yom, chag na - im nech - mad.

La la la la la la la, La la la la la la la,

Cha - nu - kah is here, Fes - ti - val of cheer. La
Cha - nu - kah ha - yom, chag na - im nech - mad.

la la la la la la la la la, La la la la la la la la la la, La

la la la la   la la la, La   la la la la la   la   la.

2 Flour, flour from the sack,
   Oil, oil from the jug,
   Let us make the pancake
   For the festival.
   La la la la la la la,
   La la la la la la la,
   Let us make the pancake
   For the festival.
   La la la la la la la la la la,
   La la la la la la la la la la,
   La la la la la la la,
   La la la la la la la.

Suggested percussion

a tambourine or any other
bright sound to accompany
the dancing

Singing game

Form the children into a circle and choose a few to
do the actions in the middle. Everyone does the
actions on the action words. The children in the
outer circle skip round to the 'la' phrases while
those in the middle pretend to finish the pancakes
and hand them round amongst themselves. After
the word 'cheer' there is a long 'la' section. Small
children can stand still and clap. Older children can
take a partner and perform a simple dance.

Potato latkes or pancakes

Organize a cooking session with the help of a
parent, preferably one who has made these
pancakes before. Have them with lunch or as an
afternoon snack. They can be fried at home if there
are no facilities at school. (See *Festival food* page 65
for recipe.)

I have got a candle   Ner li

Music by D. Sambursky, words by L. Kipnis.
Translated by Eve Benjamin.

Gently

I have got a can - dle,   It will give me light.
Nér___ li___ nér li   nér___ li da - kik

I will light my can - dle on Cha - nu - kah night. The
Ba - cha - nu - ka né - ri ad - lik

can - dle is lit for eight days long,
Ba - cha - nu - ka né - ri ya - ir

Then I can sing my Cha - nu - ka song.
Ba - cha - nu - ka shi - rim a - shir.

Movement

This can accompany the singing and is probably
more effective if it is done during a repeat of the
song. Choose eight children to carry model candles,
one each. As each line (2 bars) is sung a child walks
forward slowly and holds up one candle. The final
eight candles will represent the Menorah.

Optional accompaniments

The tune can be played by recorders and will also
sound well played on a xylophone or glockenspiel.

Banish darkness   Banu choshech

Music by Emanuel Amiran, words by Sarah Levy.
Translated by Rita Kalev

With force

Ba - nish dark-ness eve - ry - one,   We are filled with joy and song.
Ba - nu cho-shech le - ga - resh,   be - ya - de - nu or va - esh.

Each of us a light - ed torch,   Ba - nish-ing all e - vil force.
Kol e -chad hu or ka - tan,   ve - chu - la - hu or ey - tan.

Out with dark-ness, out with night,   learn ing ____ will give us light.
Su - ra cho-shech, hal - a shchor,   su - ra ____ mip - ne ha - or.

Dance

This beautiful song has a very marked persistent rhythm. It can form the basis for a circle dance similar to a traditional Israeli dance called the **horra**.

The step itself can be just a slow walk, or a slight variation of three steps forward, one step back:

left, right, left (forward), right (back), and so on.

Form the children into a circle with hands linked; older children can put their left hand onto the next child's shoulder.

line 1 – four steps to the left
line 2 – continue to the left
line 3/4 – continue but raise the right arm as if holding a torch

line 5 – face centre and walk in, arms coming down
line 6 – step back, arms opening out and up (repeat 5 and 6)

As the dance repeats and continues, the speed can increase gradually. It will finish when the children have reached their maximum speed.

Suggested percussion

    a slow drum or tambour beat

    add a tambourine

More songs about Chanukah

'Hanukkah latkes'
from *The Magic of Music Book 1* (Ginn & Co)

This is a lovely action song for younger children:

> Take a potato, pat, pat, pat,
> Roll it and make it flat, flat, flat,
> Fry in a pan with fat, fat, fat,
> Hanukkah latkes, clap, clap, clap.

'Light a little candle' is also in this collection.

'My dreydel' and 'Chanukah'
from *Music for Fun, Music for Learning* by Lois Birkenshaw (Holt, Rinehart and Winston, Canada)

Both these songs are for younger children. There are movement and percussion suggestions including some 'spinning' patterns on the xylophone.

'Chanukah song', 'Chanukah dance', 'It's Hanukah',
from *What to do until the music teacher comes* by Louise Glatt (Berandol Music Ltd, Toronto, Canada)

Three more for younger children. The first one is a counting song:

> One little candle burn, burn, burn.
> Chanukah is here.
> One little candle burn, burn, burn.
> Chanukah is here.
>
> Two little candles, etc.

The dance song has a strong rhythm and just the words:

> Hey, hey, Chanukah,
> Hey, hey, Chanukah,
> Hey, hey, Chanukah,
> Chanukah is here.

The last one is by Woodie Guthrie and can also be found in his main song collection (Ludlow Music Inc).

'Hanukkah' O Hanukkah'
from *Holiday singing and dancing games* by Esther L. Nelson (Sterling Publishing Co. Inc. New York)

This song and dance is for older children.

'In the window'
from *Silver Burdett Music Book 1* (Chester Music)

A song for older children.

Hanukah Melodies
available from J.F.N. Publishing Co, Harold Poster House, Kingsbury Circle, London NW9 9SP

This book is full of beautiful Hebrew songs – worth translating!

Poem

A play with music

My Hanukkah candles

Eight little candles
  All in a line;
Eight little candles
  Glitter and shine.

Eight little candles,
  Each little flame
Whispers a legend
  Of honour and fame.

Eight little candles,
  Sparklets of gold,
Stories of battles
  And heroes of old.

'Courage, but courage,
  Maccabee's brave son,
Fight for light –
  And the battle is
won.'

    Philip M. Raskin

The story of Chanukah

A long time ago Jewish people lived together in a land called Judea; this is called Israel today.

At the time of this story a big army of soldiers from another country called Syria marched into Judea and there was a fierce battle. The Jewish people fought bravely but the Syrians won.

The leader of the Syrians was called Antiochus – King Antiochus. He told the Jewish people that now that he was their leader, they must obey him and worship his gods. They were forbidden to worship their own God in the Temple. King Antiochus had the new laws written down and ordered his soldiers to make sure that no one disobeyed them.

The Jewish people were very unhappy because they couldn't live the way they had been used to or go to the temple to pray and to worship their own God. They thought it was wrong to worship the Syrian gods and to bow down to this new king. Many people just wouldn't obey the new laws and those who were found out were killed by the Syrian soldiers.

The people kept fighting back but couldn't drive Antiochus and his soldiers out of their land. One day they found a strong leader of their own called Judas Maccabeus, a young shepherd whose family were priests and had always hated the Syrians. They asked him to help them. 'Yes, I will lead you into battle', said Judas, 'We must beat the Syrian soldiers and turn out this cruel king.'

So Judas and his family gathered together as large an army as they could and trained them. They knew they were much smaller than the Syrian army but they were determined to win.

Then one day there was a great battle. Judas led his army riding on a horse. Antiochus led his army riding on a huge elephant. When the two leaders met everyone thought that Antiochus was safe on his elephant, but Judas knew what to do. He struck the elephant underneath its armour and killed Antiochus as he fell off the wounded animal. Judas and his army fought bravely until all the Syrian generals were killed. They won the battle. They had got rid of the Syrians.

Judas and his followers marched back to their city Jerusalem. The first thing they did was to throw out all the statues of Antiochus; then they cleaned the temple so that the people could pray there again. Everyone was very happy now that the Syrians had gone and that they could live freely again. They came to the temple to pray and to give thanks to their God. But there were no candles to burn and the oil in the temple had been spoiled by the Syrians. Suddenly one of Judas's friends, a little boy, found one small flask of pure oil, just enough to keep the lamp alight for one day. The priest said it would be eight days before any more oil would be ready. Still, they lit the lamp straight away and were amazed when, instead of going out after the first day, it burned steadily for eight days, long enough until more oil was prepared.

The Jewish people believed that this was a miracle, a special sign from their God. Every year they remember the victory of the Maccabees and celebrate the miraculous dedication of the Temple during the festival of Chanukah.

Note
It may be necessary to adapt this outline of the Chanukah story to your particular group of children and extra explanations may be needed according to their understanding or practice of religious beliefs.

To turn this story into a play you will need:
Judas Maccabeus, a shepherd, leader of the Jewish army
Antiochus, King and leader of the Syrians
The little boy who finds the flask of oil
A priest
A group of Jewish soldiers
A group of Syrian soldiers
Some Jewish families
A messenger
One or two narrators

Suggested arrangement

Scene 1
King Antiochus comes to the conquered land of Judea.

 A narrator sets the scene. Some Jewish families cross the market square going about their business when a *gong* or *cymbal* announces the arrival of

Antiochus. He tells the people that he is from Syria and that his army has conquered their land. He is now their leader and they must obey him. He orders them to erect statues of him and of his gods and says that everyone must bow down to him and to these statues. He sends a messenger to tell the people about their new laws and their new leader. Antiochus goes out leaving the families in little groups angrily discussing the news. They shake their fists at Syrian soldiers who come in to patrol and enforce the new laws.

Scene 2
The embittered Jews choose a leader and prepare for battle.

A narrator introduces. Some families meet to complain about life under Antiochus. One of them talks about the bravery of Judas the young shepherd and of his many brothers and friends who hate the Syrians. They decide to ask Judas to lead them into battle against the Syrian soldiers. A messenger is sent out and brings in Judas. He agrees to their pleadings and the men prepare for the fight.

Scene 3
The battle.

A narrator introduces. The two opposing groups meet and fight. They draw back as the two leaders meet. Antiochus is killed. The Judeans cheer as the Syrian soliders turn to escape. Judas tells his followers that they must march back to Jerusalem to tell the people.

Scene 4
The miracle of the burning oil.

 A narrator introduces. The people are huddled in the market square. A *drum* beats in the returning victorious army and a *gong* or *cymbal* brings in Judas. He tells the news. There is a great cheer and the families greet the soldiers. Judas orders the throwing out of all the Syrian statues and asks for volunteers to clean the temple so that they can give thanks to their God. Everyone scrubs, cleans and polishes. Judas says that there are no candles and that all the oil has been spoilt. While everyone discusses what to do and some look around, a small boy brings a flask of pure oil to Judas. He shows it to a priest who says that it will burn for one day only and that it will be at least eight days before more oil can be prepared. Judas and the priest agree to light the flask.

Everyone kneels while this is done. They all go out. (The children can *hum* the tune of 'Drive out darkness everyone' slowly and quietly to indicate the passing of the days. A *gong, cymbal* or *low D chime bar* can sound at the end of each of the eight bars.)

Everyone re-enters and draws back in amazement when they see the little flask of oil still burning. They kneel. The narrator (or Judas) comes forward and explains that the miracle of the oil burning for eight days was taken to be a special sign from the God of the Jews and that ever since the festival of Chanukah has been celebrated every year. He shows a model of a Menorah and explains that the candles are lit in a special way, the first day one candle, the second day two candles, and so on. Everyone stands up and sings the song 'Drive out darkness everyone'.

Suggested music

The opening bars of Handel's overture to *Judas Maccabeus* can be used to set the beginning scene and to accompany some of the movement of dejected family groups in this scene and Scene Two. *Drums, clappers* and *a cymbal* can be used for the battle scene. The last part of Handel's overture can be used in Scene Four as the people return to find the flask of oil still burning. It could also be used as well as (or instead of) the last song to conclude the play.

Costume ideas for the play

These sketches provide a basis for improvised costumes from sheeting, curtains, clean, cast off adult clothes and items from the school wardrobe. It is often sufficient to use headgear only and a few props such as spears, axes and shields for the soldiers.

Jewish soldier   *Syrian soldier*

Jewish woman   *High Priest*

Little boy

Judas Maccabeus   *Antiochus, the Syrian King*

Background information

Christmas, or the Mass of Christ, is one of the two most important festivals in the Christian year when the birth of the baby Jesus is celebrated. The other is Easter, his death and resurrection.

Christmas Day always falls on December 25th. It is the beginning of a break of about three days and comes in the school holidays at the end of the Autumn term. It is not known when the birth of Jesus actually took place but it is thought that it was probably in the winter time during the reign of the Roman Emperor Augustus. The choice of this particular mid-winter day enabled the first Christians to celebrate at the same time as the ancient pagans were feasting the Winter Solstice, and there is no doubt that a holiday coming at the time of the shortest working days and the worst weather would have been most welcome. As Christianity spread these festivals were gradually merged under the wing of the church, so it is not surprising that many of our Christmas customs can be traced back to pre-Christian times.

We associate the evergreens, holly, ivy and mistletoe with Christmas and we use them to decorate our houses and Christmas food. The holly and the ivy are linked in many seasonal songs.

> The holly and the ivy,
> When they are both full grown,
> Of all the trees that are in the wood
> The holly bears the crown.

Holly was thought to be lucky and to cure fevers and rheumatism. Christians associate it with the crown of thorns worn by Jesus on the cross and the red berries with the blood that he shed. Many people adopt the American custom of hanging a holly wreath on their front door at Christmas. The mistletoe was considered sacred by the Druids. An old Norse legend features it as a symbol of love, but it could also be that this association came from the growing of the berries in pairs. We now use it as an excuse for kissing!

The tradition of the decorated fir or Christmas tree is a relatively recent one in this country. It became popular when Prince Albert, husband of Queen Victoria, brought it with him from Germany. Now most homes, schools and public buildings display a brightly coloured tree during the Christmas season. The famous one in Trafalgar Square is an annual gift from the people of Oslo and is the centre of attraction for visitors to London.

Candles are another Christmas decoration but because of fire hazard, coloured lights take their place on the Christmas tree. In pre-Christian times they were linked with the heat and light of the sun which was to regain strength with the return of the longer days. To Christians they symbolize the light and truth of Jesus and his teachings. Lights are an important feature of other religious festivals – Diwali and Chanukah, for instance.

The legend of Father Christmas or Santa Claus can be traced back to a real Saint Nicholas, a much loved bishop who lived in Myra, Asia Minor. He was a generous man who loved both poor people and children. He died on December 6th and in some countries children receive their Christmas presents on December 5th, the eve of his festival.

Christmas is celebrated in different ways among the many Christian communities in the world. In this country Christmas Eve is a day of great excitement when preparations for Christmas Day itself are finalized. Carol singers pay their last visits, children hang up their stockings and there are midnight services in church. Christmas Day is usually a family occasion for most people. There are frequently special Christmas services, then the main meal of the festival is taken in the early afternoon; a feast of turkey or other roast fowl, roast potatoes, Christmas pudding and mince pies.

Christmas is a joyous time for children all over the world – a truly international festival. The choice of the carols and songs in this section reflects this and the suggested Christmas play can be interpreted as the climax of a general theme of 'Children in other countries'. Thus it can become an integral part of a topic-based curriculum which would be minimally splintered when Christmas activities are introduced; it could occupy the second half of the Autumn term. The songs themselves should be introduced well ahead so that there is time for everyone, including the children, to consider words, choose verses and make a final selection. There should also be an opportunity for all the children to take part in all the movement and dances before the characters and groups are eventually agreed. Thus the final putting together will benefit from the earlier involvement of the children.

The Christmas play

Suggested presentation

All the children can be seated in a large semi-circle which faces the scene set to receive Mary, Joseph, the shepherds, kings and angels. This can be as simple or elaborate as each school chooses. The groups of children who bring gifts to the manger can sit with the others or enter from the side according to the arrangements of each school. Everyone sings.

CAROL	MOVEMENT
Beth'lem lay a-sleeping (Polish)	Mary and Joseph walk in slowly to the 'stable'. Mary puts the baby in the manger. (The angels enter.)
Under Beth'lem's stars so bright (Czech)	The shepherds enter one by one, give their gifts and take their places.
The gifts (Swedish)	The wise men enter one by one, give their gifts and take their places.
What shall I give to the child in the manger? (Spanish)	Two groups of children enter carrying baskets of fruit. They give the fruit to Mary and sit down.
Bom bom bom (Chilean)	A group of children enters. Two of them give a pair of tiny red shoes to Mary. The others peep at the baby and sit down.
Baby Jesus I sing to you (Brazilian)	A group of younger children enters, dances and sits down.
The children's band (South Carolina)	Enter children playing instruments. They play and dance, then sit down.
Lullaby: Sleep, pretty one (Modern)	Everyone sings quietly.
Girls and boys, leave your toys (Czech) *Child for the world* (Modern)	Both these carols provide a suitable finale to the play. Teachers of younger children may prefer to omit the Czech carol. During the singing a few gifts of toys can be taken to the manger. The audience may enjoy joining in the chorus.

These suggestions can be very easily modified: some carols can be omitted while others can be added if they slot in with the theme. Readings and/or dialogue can be introduced to suit individual settings. Here is an opportunity for encouragement and practice in reading distinctly, and teachers should emphasize that this is as important as the acting parts. Full movement suggestions can be found in the notes to each carol.

Costumes

The costuming of the children can arise out of a general study of clothes in other countries if this is introduced early enough in the term. Get the children to bring in any costumed dolls they may have (take great care of them) and books too. Stock up the classroom library with suitably illustrated and informative books. These could extend the study to include customs, houses and weather.

Every single child can be costumed as simply or as elaborately as you decide. The costuming of the children taking part in the tableau will look better if it is uniform, otherwise each child can virtually please himself.

I found costuming to be one of the most enjoyable aspects of this particular Christmas 'offering'. Many parents helped, especially with the groups; among the children a great deal of speculation, improvisation and invention went on. The result was a blaze of colour when they all assembled; a very warm sight to brighten the greyness of a winter's day.

Mary, Joseph, the shepherds and the kings can be dressed traditionally according to the school wardrobe. Here are some suggestions for simple costumes for the groups who enter to form the final tableau:

Girls can wear a blouse and fairly long skirt and sandals. A scarf can be worn in 'manto' style, draped over the head and around the face, neck and shoulders. Otherwise they can wear plenty of jewellery and ear rings.

Boys can dress as a Chilean cowboy or *huaso*. The trousers, pin-striped if possible, are tied around with a ribbon or band in imitation of the traditional leather leggins. A shirt, loose waistcoat and round felt hat complete the outfit.

The population of Chile consists of Indians, European immigrants and mixed races and western style dress has been adapted.

Spanish girl   *Spanish boy*

Girls can wear a blouse, coloured skirt, apron, shawl and a flower in their hair. White tights and black shoes. Earrings.

Boys can wear a white shirt, black trousers, waistcoat (bolero type) red cummerbund and a red head band (optional). Black shoes.

Chilean girl   *Chilean boy*

Brazilian girl   *Brazilian boy*

Girls can wear a white frilly blouse, long or short floral patterned skirt, necklaces, ear rings, socks and sandals.

Boys can wear a long sleeved shirt, sleeveless waistcoat, black or grey loose trousers tucked into boots, a coloured scarf around the neck and a wide brimmed felt hat. This is the dress of a Gaucho ranchhand (cattle breeder).

There are many different racial and ethnic groups in Brazil; immigrants have adapted their own national costumes to the climate of their new country.

The children from *South Carolina* can wear clothes similar to our own summer dress, but not too 'dressy'.

It can be argued that the action takes place in the winter at the time of the birth of Jesus and that the costume should reflect this. When I was involved with this little Christmas play a more symbolic point of view was taken. Again the children can be dressed more correctly as children – in ordinary clothes. Teachers will make their own interpretations and adapt their setting accordingly.

Language

When each child or group of children has decided what costume to wear for the Christmas play, simple research into the way of life, weather and customs of that country can be encouraged. Each child can imagine that he or she is coming from that country; they could choose names for themselves, write a story about their life there and draw pictures of their costumes. Individual booklets or class folders could display this work.

Art and craft

Classroom and corridor friezes and collages can all reflect the theme of children from other countries. The hall, where the celebration is taking place, can be decorated with paintings and pictures, perhaps showing the lands represented by the children in the tableau. A German Advent Wreath could form a central hanging piece.

Musical mobiles

Hang some musical mobiles over the music corner. Make them with wire coat hangers, foil cake cups and silver tinsel.

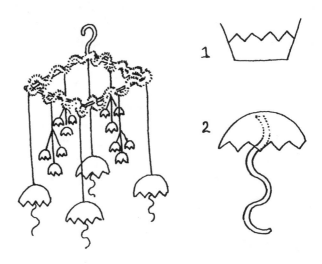

1 Cut round a foil cake cup with pinking scissors.
2 Shape into a bell by pressing over a lemon squeezer or small bowl. Fix cut strip to hang from centre of bell.
3 Hang prepared bells at different levels with cotton and decorate mobile with tinsel.

Christmas crackers

Make Christmas crackers from toilet roll holders, crepe paper and shiny string. Put Christmas messages inside and decorate the outside. Cut the ends and pull to shape.

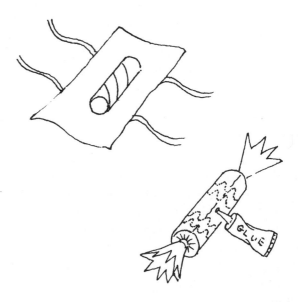

Christmas trees

Make Christmas trees from cotton reels, plastic milk straws and circles of green coloured paper. Glue the straw into the cotton reel base (painted or decorated beforehand) and slide the leafy circles carefully down the straw starting with bigger circles at the bottom. Secure with a dab of glue if necessary and spray with glitter.

There are a fascinating variety of ways of making trees outlined in Jean Chapman's *The Sugar-Plum Christmas Book* (Hodder and Stoughton).

Nativity scene

Make a nativity scene set in a large carton. Figures can be made from toilet roll holders or squeezy containers cut in half. Each child could make a model of him or herself in his or her chosen costume so that the complete model would represent the Christmas play.

Christmas cards

These are a 'must'. No doubt this theme will inspire drawings and designs. Don't forget the local hospital children's ward, old people's homes, the lollipop man or lady, the children's library and any other local children's groups. Large cards in the style of a group collage might be good for these. Encourage good or 'special' writing and concentrate on attractive presentation. Don't leave until the last minute!

Festival food and customs

Food is an important part of all festivals, not least the festival of Christmas. It is part of a general pattern of celebrations, a pattern which has interesting variations from country to country. The notes in this section describe aspects of food and customs in the countries featured in the carol selection.

Poland

In *Poland* holiday fasting ends with the first star on Christmas Eve. The head of the household breaks an **oplatek**, a large, thin, consecrated wafer, with each person and exchanges wishes for their health and happiness. These wafers are baked in cast-iron moulds stamped with pictures of the nativity and blessed by the priest. In rural areas wafers are divided among cattle, horses and sheep.

The Christmas Eve supper, the **Wilia**, sometimes includes an extra place at the table for any stranger who might knock. Traditionally a thirteen-course meal in memory of Christ and the twelve apostles would be prepared. It would begin with a classic soup, *borsch* (beetroot), mushroom or almond. Several kinds of fish dishes would follow – the famous carp (or pike) with gingersnap sauce was popular – accompanied by vegetables such as Old Polish peas with cabbage and dishes from dried mushrooms. Finally, there would be a wheat or rice based dessert with honey sauce followed by a variety of preserves, confections and small honey and poppy-seed cakes.

Today the supper is less lavish but will reflect the culinary traditions. The Christmas tree stands decorated with coloured candles, nuts, apples, homemade ornaments and (blown) decorated eggs. In some places the Good Star from Heaven, a woman with a white dress and flowing veil, brings presents for the children.

Czechoslovakia

Christmas for children in *Czechoslovakia* begins on December 5th, the Eve of the festival of Saint Nicholas, when they receive presents of apples, nuts and candies. About this time young boys go around the village with 'wooden snakes', little flexible playthings cut out of wood and carved with the head of a snake. They go from house to house singing carols while one of the boys waves the snake and in return they receive a gift. In some villages shepherds visit houses with their bag-pipes and a group of singers.

A holiday fast, observed by many families, is broken when the first star appears on Christmas Eve, known as 'Starry evening'. There is usually a layer of snow already covering the ground lending an atmosphere to this time when young people amuse themselves with old charms and spells. Girls shake the lilac tree and chant, 'Lilac, lilac tree, I pray you tell me where my love may be'. Mothers slice an apple crosswise 'for luck' for their children; a core with a perfect star means happiness. Fortunes are told from movements of nutshells fitted with lighted tapers floating inside a tub of water.

Families sit down to a traditional supper, the main meal of the holiday. This will include roe soup, fish (usually carp) prepared in a variety of ways with potato salad, special shaped breads and holiday cake with almonds and raisins. Afterwards the family gathers round a glittering Christmas tree to sing or listen to carols. Under the tree will be presents for everyone from Santa Claus. Christmas Day itself is a quiet family holiday.

Sweden

In *Sweden* the Christmas season lasts a month from December 13, Saint Lucia's Day until January 13, Saint Knut's Day. On December 13 young daughters in a household act the part of Saint Lucia, Queen of Light. Dressed in white and wearing a crown of greenery studded with candles, they wake the rest of the family in the early morning with a tray of coffee and newly baked Lucia buns. Often a candlelight procession will go round neighbouring houses. Christmas preparations now being in earnest, houses are spring-cleaned, presents are bought or made and special foods are prepared. These include the **lutefisk**, dried cod which has to be soaked for fourteen days. It is then boiled and can be served with a white sauce and potatoes or with melted butter and lingonberry sauce.

On Christmas Eve the family gathers round a big kettle or iron pot for the ceremony of 'dipping the kettle'. The 'dip' is a thick broth made from sausages, pork and corned beef. Everyone spears a piece of bread on a fork, dips in and eats the saturated bread with a piece of meat. The family then move into the dining room for luncheon which is usually an array of smörgåsbord or appetizers and lutfisk, sometimes followed by ham and usually finishing with rice pudding. Whoever finds the one hidden almond will marry within a year! After this comes the lighting of the candles on the Christmas tree, carols, present giving and a visit from Jultomtem, Sweden's Santa Claus.

Spain

Christmas Eve, or Nochebuena, is the time for an elaborate fair in many parts of *Spain*. Toys, marzipan flowers, fruit, all kinds of food and small wooden or plaster figures for nativity scenes can be bought. Midnight Mass interrupts the festivities – but only temporarily, for street dancing goes on until dawn. Christmas dinner is a family occasion and is eaten very late in the evening. A typical dinner may consist of turkey, roast sucking pig, or roast lamb, followed by all kinds of sweetmeats such as **turron**, a kind of nougat, crystallized fruits, toasted almonds and nuts.

Although it is quite common these days for presents to be given at Christmas, the children do not get their presents from Santa Claus but, traditionally, from the Three Wise Men as they travel through Spain on their way to Bethlehem. The night before Epiphany, January 6, young people stuff hay or grain into their shoes and leave them on the balcony for the Wise Men's camels (or horses). In the morning the food is always gone and cakes, candies and toys are left in its place. Epiphany begins in many cities with a colourful procession of the Magi Kings. At Palma the Kings arrive by torchlight led by a city official on horseback. At Las Palmas they arrive by camel. At Alicante when I was there they came by boat.

Chile

Chile is a Spanish speaking country extending north-south along the western seaboard of South America. Christmas comes in the summer time, but for many families means little more than a carefully cooked meal because of the poverty that afflicts much of the country. There will be a nativity scene in homes that can house such a model and a Christmas tree for those who can afford it. A Midnight Mass is held on Christmas Eve and Christmas Day itself will be spent in holiday fashion. The Christmas meal will include any kind of salad, special creamy cakes and chocolate-type biscuits. There are fairs or fiestas in many parts with big displays of national crafts: handmade rugs, blankets and jewellery.

Brazil

Christmas in *Brazil* comes in midsummer at the

beginning of the long school holidays. It is not surprising, therefore, that many of the celebrations are open-air. The original Portuguese-Catholic observances have been modified by African, Indian and other influences, so Christmas celebrations and customs take many forms. There are elaborate pageants, singing, dancing, folk plays and satirical dramas. An example of the latter is the 'Bumba-meu-boi' (Whoa, my ox). It consists of a series of sketches involving the death of an ox, a play complete with a villain, a doctor, a priest, and a hobgoblin, and lasts from Christmas until Epiphany. There is also the Festival of the Three Kings and dance festivals such as the Fandango and the Cheganca, sometimes accompanied by the lighting of bonfires and firework displays.

The traditional Christmas is kept in larger cities among Christian communities. There is usually an elaborate nativity scene set up in the home. Families attend church at midnight on Christmas Eve and return home to a dinner of roast pig, probably steamed fish pie and various exotic desserts. The bringer of presents is Santa Claus (known as Papai Noel), who still comes dressed in his red arctic suit.

U.S.A.

Christmas in the United States is a collage of customs brought by its people from all over the world. *South Carolina* is one of the fourteen states comprising the vast region known as the Deep South. Here, in the land of the big plantations, well cooked holiday meals were important. Traditionally Christmas Eve was a time for reflective prayers and hymn singing, but the Christmas spirit took over as the first cock crowed and the dancing, feasting and singing of the seven-day festival began. Today, the Christmas season reflects the noise and gaiety of earlier times.

Here is a small selection of Christmas recipes from other countries to try.

A Christingle (from Germany)

This is an orange, decorated to represent various aspects of the Christian belief. The custom of giving a Christingle to every member of the congregation at the Christmas Eve service was started in the eighteenth century by the Moravian church in Saxony and still survives today.

To make a Christingle slice a piece off the bottom of an orange so that it stands firm, fix a candle in its

holder into the top and decorate the base with a small red crepe paper frill. Put sweets, nuts and raisins on to one end of a cocktail stick and secure the other end into the orange around the frill at the base of the candle.

The orange represents the world and the sweets, nuts and raisins symbolize the animals and fruits of the earth. The red frill represents the blood of Christ; the candle itself stands for the Light of the World.

Mincemeat cookies (from the USA)

100g (4 oz) butter or margarine
100g (4 oz) brown sugar
150g (6 oz) mincemeat
200g (8 oz) plain flour
1 egg
½ teaspoon bicarbonate soda
½ teaspoon salt
2 teaspoons lemon juice

METHOD
1 Cream butter and sugar together.
2 Beat the egg well and add to mixture.
3 Add mincemeat and lemon.
4 Mix flour and bicarbonate soda and sieve into mixture. Mix well.
5 Drop teaspoons of mixture on to greased baking tin to make about three or four dozen cookies.
6 Bake in a moderate oven, gas mark 5 (375°F, 190°C) for 10 minutes.

Saffron bread (from Sweden)

Most families in Sweden bake saffron bread for the day of Santa Lucia, December 13th, and have it available until Christmas is over. It is a light spongy yeasted cake, tastes very good when freshly baked and is usually served with afternoon tea or coffee.

1 level teaspoon sugar
50 ml (2 tablespoons) hot, not boiling, water
2 tablespoons dried yeast
400g (1 lb) strong plain white flour
2 level teaspoons salt
50g (2 oz) soft butter

50g (2 oz) sugar
25g (1 oz) seedless raisins/sultanas
200 ml (1 teacup) lukewarm milk
1 level teaspoon saffron powder (mix with about
1 tablespoon hot water)
Beaten egg for final brushing

Topping
1 tablespoon flaked almonds
1 tablespoon sugar (preferably caster)

METHOD
1 Dissolve one teaspoon sugar in hot water, stir in yeast and leave until frothy.
2 Sift flour and salt into a bowl, rub in butter and add sugar and raisins/sultanas.
3 Mix to a dough with yeast mixture, milk and saffron powder. Knead thoroughly with extra flour if necessary, shape into a ball, cover and leave in a warm place to rise.
4 When dough is doubled in size, turn out on to floured surface, 'punch down', kneading quickly and lightly.
5 Divide dough into three (or six) equal pieces, roll each into a long sausage shape about 40 cm (or 20 cm) long and plait together making one large or two smaller loaves. Alternatively just shape into a loaf. Cover and leave in a warm place until doubled in size.
6 Brush with beaten egg and sprinkle with sugar and almonds.
7 Bake in a hot oven, gas 6 (200°C/400°F) for about ½ hour or until golden brown.
8 Cool and eat while fresh.

I found saffron difficult to get and then very expensive. I made the bread without it. The result was still delicious though not true saffron bread. The children enjoyed it with butter. Two days later it toasted very well.

Jamaican gingerbread

2 teaspoons powdered ginger
300g (12 oz) plain flour
50g (2 oz) chopped mixed candied peel
100g (4 oz) butter or margarine
200g (8 oz) molasses
½ teaspon bicarbonate soda
4 tablespoons warm milk
2 well beaten eggs
100g (4 oz) sugar

To decorate
Candied peel

METHOD
1 Sift the flour and ginger, add peel and mix.
2 Heat sugar, butter and molasses over a low heat until the sugar dissolves.
3 Dissolve the bicarbonate of soda in the milk, add the beaten eggs and beat a little more.
4 Add this mixture to the flour and mix thoroughly.
5 Line a square cake tin with greaseproof paper, fill it with the mixture and bake in a slow oven, gas mark 2 (300°F) for 1¾ hours.
6 Cool on rack. Decorate the top of the cake with thin slices of candied peel. Cut into small slices.

There are many suitable recipes among Herbert Wernecke's excellent collection in *Christmas Customs around the World*.

Sound pictures

Winter weather can be a good subject for sound pictures. They will be mainly impressionistic, but if you can provide some good pictures to stimulate the children's imagination, it is surprising how effective they can be. They won't and shouldn't last long, of course, unless the children themselves are inventive enough to vary and sustain their playing.

Here are some suggestions, but remember to build on the children's ideas and use this opportunity to develop language:

grey skies
stroke or scratch the head of a tambour or drum; wobble a ruler or strip of card over the sound hole of two or three chime bars. Choose low ones that are close together in pitch like C, C♯, D

cold, frost
trill a triangle
'shimmer' a cymbal with a padded beater
quietly rattle finger cymbals together

snow
quiet shakers
milk bottle tops in a paper bag

people skating
slide a beater up and down a xylophone or glockenspiel;
swanee whistle

rain

gentle – shakers or rice rolled on top of a drum or tambour;
heavier – tambourine or clappers
(It is a good idea for the children to actually *listen* to rain on a suitable occasion.)

dull, muggy weather

slide up and down ('glissando') over two or three low notes on a glockenspiel or metallophone; against this play a few random notes quietly on an alto xylophone.

mist, light fog

humming which 'wanders' between two or three notes; very soft shakers come and go.

wind

voices *sh-w-sh-w-sh mmmmmmmmmm*

Possible approaches:

1 It is the beginning of afternoon playtime in a city school. It is a dull, muggy day and a damp mist is just visible. The traffic rumbles in the High Road; an aeroplane crosses out of sight; the street lights come on. A few children come out buttoning up their coats; then a few more – then several classes spill out with noisy chatter.

2 You wake up one morning to see a white covering everywhere; snow is falling gently; the birds fly down to look for food.

3 You decide to go out for some slides in the snow. Your footsteps crunch in the crisp white snow. Your friends join you and you play snowballs on the way. You find a place where other people are sliding and join in. It begins to snow heavily so everyone has a last slide and goes home.

e.g. using notes E G A:

My name is Carlos.   I come from Mexico.

Sound pictures

If your children have enjoyed making winter weather sound pictures, leave out the instruments you have used so that small groups of children can follow up this activity by creating their own sound impressions. Link with painting. Display good illustrations and the children's pictures.

Music corner

Making up tunes

This can be linked with the children's work to do with children in other countries. It has been suggested that they choose a name for themselves to go with the costume they are to be dressed in for the Christmas play. Every child could then make up a tune based on two simple sentences:

My name is (Carlos).
I come from (Mexico).

Carol

Polish folk tune, words by Francis B. Wood. Adapted by Jean Gilbert

2 Angels sweetly singing,
   Long, so long ago;
   Sending praises ringing,
   Long, so long ago.
   Children too their love may bring
   To baby Jesus born a king,
   So long, long ago.

Suggested percussion

A single triangle to accompany the lines:
   Twinkling stars were peeping,
   Long, so long ago.

Sing this carol very gently. It can provide a suitably quiet opening to the songs and movement that follow. Begin by humming the tune through. Mary and Joseph enter during the singing of the first verse and sit down in the centre of the tableau. The second verse is optional but can provide an entry for the angels if you are going to include them. Any further movement such as Mary settling the baby in the manger can be supported by humming.

Under Bethl'em's stars so bright

Czech traditional carol

Gaily

VERSE
C

p

1. Un - der Beth-l'em's

stars so bright, Shep - herds watched their flocks by night.

CHORUS

Hy - dom, hy - dom, tid - li - dom, Hy - dom, hy - dom

Last time

tid - li - dom.

pp

2 Came an angel telling them,
   They must go to Bethlehem.
   CHORUS

3 'Hasten, hasten,' they did say,
   'Jesus Christ you'll find that way.'
   CHORUS

4 'Sleeping in a manger bare
   Lies the holy child so fair.'
   CHORUS

5 'Mary rocks him tenderly,
   Joseph sings a lullaby.'
   CHORUS

Christmas is still one of the most important festivals of the year in a Czech village. As it draws near mystery plays may be performed. Traditionally Christmas Eve was the time when each house would be visited by the village shepherd with his bagpipes and a group of singers.

Optional chimes

The following 'drone' will give the effect of bagpipes:

Suggested percussion

drum or tambour beat on the chorus

Movement

This is a good carol to provide an entry for the shepherds. They can begin to enter on the third verse, quietly give their gifts and take their places in the tableau by the fifth verse. The singing should quieten in the last two verses and the carol could end with humming once through the tune.

Playing by ear

When your children know the tune well, leave out chimes C D E F and a simple work card to help them try the chorus:

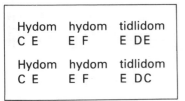

Hydom	hydom	tidlidom
C E	E F	E DE
Hydom	hydom	tidlidom
C E	E F	E DC

Guitar can play in a higher key for older children. Use key D throughout. Chimes for the drone are then D and A.

The gifts

Swedish melody, words by June Witham

2 That star led them to Beth'lem
   Where Baby Jesus lay;
   The new-born king was sleeping,
   In borrowed bed of hay,
   The new-born king was sleeping
   In borrowed bed of hay.

3 Those wise men knelt and worshipped
   In praise at Jesu's birth,
   And we our hearts now offer,
   We sing with joyous mirth:
   For Mary's child – and God's Son –
   Has come to save the earth.

Suggested percussion

drum or tambour with a padded beater

Movement

Sung at a steady pace this song gives a good rhythm
for the entry of the wise men. They could enter
singly as the three verses proceed.

What shall I give to the child in the manger?

Spanish traditional carol arranged by
Angela Diller and Kate Stearns Page

Clearly and rhythmically

2 What shall I give
   To the child in the manger?
   What shall I give
   To the beautiful boy?
      Garlands of flowers
      To twine in his fingers,
      Cherries so big
      For the child to enjoy.
   Tam - pa - tam - tam
      When the cherries have ripened,
   Tam - pa - tam - tam
      They will add to his joy.

Suggested percussion

tambourine
or side drum

or
more simply

Movement

Two groups of children can enter bringing in the
fruits mentioned in the two verses. A few of them
can put the fruit by the manger while the rest skip
round in a circle to 'Tam-pa-tam-tam . . .'

Bom bom bom

Chilean children's carol

Gently and smoothly

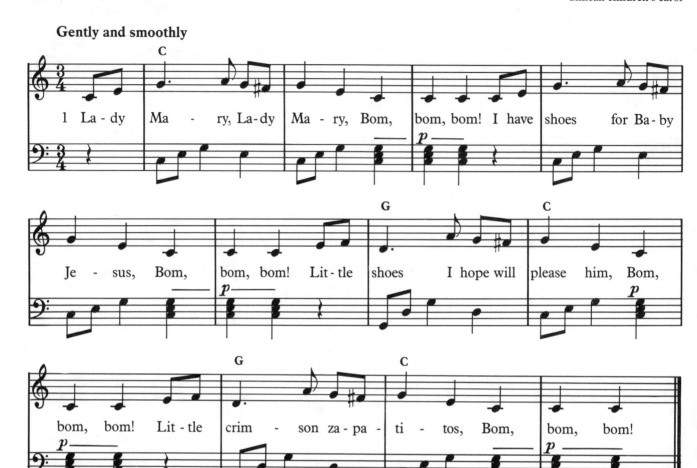

2 Lady Mary, Lady Mary,
Bom, bom, bom!
I have come across the city,
Bom, bom, bom!
Come to see the holy family,
Bom, bom, bom!
In the stable hushed and pretty,
Bom, bom, bom!

3 Lady Mary, Lady Mary,
Bom, bom, bom!
There's a mouse inside the manger,
Bom, bom, bom!
See, he's nibbling at the donkey,
Bom, bom, bom!
Do you like the little stranger?
Bom, bom, bom!

Suggested percussion

triangle or finger cymbals

drum or tambour

(bom, bom, bom)

Movement

This is a song for younger children. Let a small group process behind one or two children who carry some tiny red shoes to give to Mary. The step is a slow walking one, though some children might manage a variation as if to show off their shoes: *step left, point right foot* and *rest; step right, point left foot* and *rest;* count *1 2 3* and so on.

Baby Jesus I sing to you

Brazilian clapping song arranged by Shirley Winfield,
words adapted by Jean Gilbert

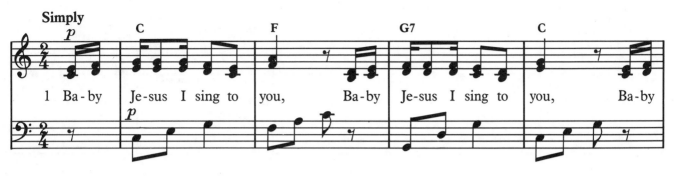

1 Ba-by Je-sus I sing to you, Ba-by Je-sus I sing to you, Ba-by

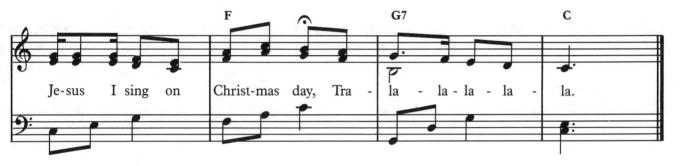

Je-sus I sing on Christ-mas day, Tra - la - la-la-la - la.

2 Baby Jesus, I play to you,
   Baby Jesus, I play to you,
   Baby Jesus, I play on Christmas day,
   Tra - la - la - la - la - la.

3 Baby Jesus, I dance for you,
   Baby Jesus, I dance for you,
   Baby Jesus, I dance on Christmas day,
   Tra - la - la - la - la - la.

4 Baby Jesus, I bring my love,
   Baby Jesus, I bring my love,
   Baby Jesus, I bring my love to you,
   Mm - mm - mm - mm - mm - mm.

Suggested percussion

A tambourine can accompany the claps at the end of
the first two lines in every verse.

Movement

This is a lovely song for the very young children.
They could enter simply singing 'Baby Jesus, I
come to you' and then form a circle for the
appropriate actions for each verse; one or two
children might be chosen to do these actions while
the rest sing. It will depend upon the group.

The children's band

Traditional song from South Carolina, adapted by Jean Gilbert

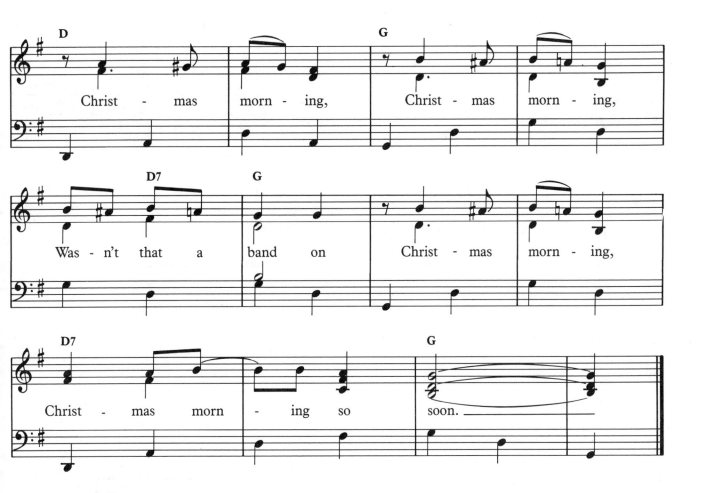

Christ - mas morn - ing, Christ - mas morn - ing,

Was - n't that a band on Christ - mas morn - ing,

Christ - mas morn - ing so soon.

2 The bells are going to ring on Christmas morning,
   Christmas morning, Christmas morning,
   The bells are going to ring on Christmas morning,
   Christmas morning so soon.

This traditional song from South Carolina (known also as 'The angel band') was sung in rural churches where the congregation would improvise the verses collectively. There were no hymn books, due either to poverty or illiteracy, and so most of the songs were simple and could be sung this way.

Suggested percussion

On chorus:

tambour

cymbal, tapped with a stick

Optional chimes

Verse 2

glockenspiel, chime bars, metallophone or recorders

Sleep, pretty one

Sewah Amponsem (Michael Faraday School, London)

VERSE **Simply**

Je - sus, oh Je - sus, oh you're ___ so mild, and the
Oh you are such ___ a pret - ty child, and the

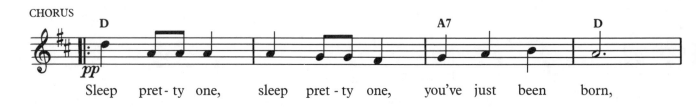

an - gels are sing - ing a - bove. ___
an - gels they give you their love. ___

CHORUS

Sleep pret - ty one, sleep pret - ty one, you've just been born,

Sleep pret - ty one, sleep pret - ty one, this Christ - mas morn.

Optional accompaniment

Play quietly in the style of a drone on chimes,
glockenspiel or metallophone.

Girls and boys, leave your toys

Czech folk tune, words by Malcolm Sargent

2   On that day, far away,
    Jesus lay,
    Angeles were watching round his head.
    Holy child, mother mild,
    undefiled,

We sing thy praise.
'Hallelujah' the church bells ring
'Hallelujah' the angels sing,
'Hallelujah' from everything.
All must draw near.

Child for the world

Words and music by David Medd

With expression

1 Ly - ing in a man-ger, ___ Ox ___ and ass be - side,

Man ___ a-bove the man-ger, ___ Watch - ing with his bride: ___ A

lit - tle boy lay on the straw, ___ Sleep - ing in the hay,

CHORUS

And an - gels sang a song for him, ___ born ___ on Christ-mas Day, Yes

an - gels sang a song for him, ___ born ___ on Christ-mas Day.

More carols for Christmas

2 In the fall of winter,
Out beside the stream,
Lying in a wigwam
In the silver beam;
The tribes around brought rabbit skins
And coloured beads to play,

CHORUS

3 In the summer sunlight,
Down below the hill,
With palms above Him
The seawind sleeping still,
A little boy lay in the sand;
The sea-birds watched Him play,

CHORUS

4 In the smoky city,
In the foggy street,
Mist around the houses,
Water at your feet;
'A boy is born at No. 4,'
I heard the milkman say,

CHORUS

The Cuckoo Carol (Czech)
Lindsay Carol Book 1 (Lindsay Music)

Children's Song of the Nativity (English)
More Carols with Chimes Rees/Mendoza (O.U.P.)

Patapan (Burgundian Drum Carol)
Carols with Chimes Rees/Mendoza (O.U.P.)

I'm a little Indian (Ecuador)
Sociable Carols Mendoza/Shaw (O.U.P.)

Bell Carol (Czech)
Sociable Carols Mendoza/Shaw (O.U.P.)

The Orchestra Carol (Czech)
Sociable Carols Mendoza/Shaw (O.U.P.)

Rocking (Czech)
Carols with Chimes Rees/Mendoza (O.U.P.)

We are going to the stable (Czech)
The International Book of Christmas Carols (Prentice-Hall)

Come, they told me, parum pum pum pum (Czech)
Carol, gaily carol (A. & C. Black)

There were three kings (Flemish)
Carol, gaily carol (A. & C. Black)

O come, little children (Modern)
Carol, gaily carol (A. & C. Black)

March of the kings (French)
Merrily to Bethlehem (A. & C. Black)

This lovely little modern song can provide a very suitable ending to this group of songs (an alternative ending to 'Girls and boys, leave your toys'), as it relates Christ's birth to Christmas births at other times and places.

Sing the verses quietly, concentrating on the words, and build up on the chorus.

Suggested percussion

A single tambourine to boost the chorus:

Poems

Some Christmas riddles

Flour of England, fruit of Spain,
Met together in a shower of rain;
Put in a bag tied round with a string;
If you tell me this riddle,
I'll give you a ring.

(Plum pudding)

I'm called by the name of a man,
Yet I am as little as a mouse;
When winter comes I love to be
With my red target near a house.

(A robin)

Highty, tighty, paradighty,
Clothed all in green,
The king could not read it,
No more could the queen;
They sent for the wise men
From out of the East,
Who said it had horns,
But was not a beast.

(A holly-leaf)

Anon

I like Christmas

I'm sure that I like Christmas the best
Of any time
In all the year.

I like to help bring loads of greens
And put them up
For Christmas cheer.

I like to open packages
And help prepare
Good things to eat.

Or go a-caroling at night
With all my friends
Along the street.

I like to think of Santa Claus
And help to decorate
Our Tree.

Yes, I am sure that Christmas is
The best time
Of the year for me.

James S. Tippett

Christmas

My goodness, my goodness,
It's Christmas again.
The bells are all ringing.
I do not know when
I've been so excited.
The tree is all fixed,
The candles are lighted,
The pudding is mixed.

The wreath's on the door
And the carols are sung,
The presents are wrapped
And the holly is hung.
The turkey is sitting
All safe in its pan,
And I am behaving
As calm as I can.

Marchette Chute

Sound poem

Christmas in two lands

There it is cold, or there is snow –
And holly, fires and mistletoe,
And carols sung out in the street
By children, walking through the sleet.
Church bells break the frozen air
Ringing loudly everywhere.
There is where white winter glory
Comes to tell the Christmas story.

Here it is hot, the sun is gold –
And turns tired when day is old,
Christmas carols are sung at night
Somewhere outside, by candle-light.
Church bells ring out in the heat
And call to people in the street.
The Christmas story here is told
In summer, when the sun is gold.

Joan Mellings

This poem could stimulate some discussion among the children about Christmas in other countries. Can they solve the puzzle about where 'here' is?

The poem describes aspects of the weather in a hot and cold country at the time of Christmas. Ask the children to describe in more detail what really

cold winter weather is like and what they remember of really hot weather. Now try sound pictures creating impressions in sound based on the children's descriptions. Here are some questions to build on:

There it is cold	**Suggested sounds**
frost	trill a triangle 'shiver' finger cymbals
snow	quiet shakers
biting wind	cymbal shimmered with a padded beater – voices
grey skies	gently tap a tambour or drum head with a padded beater

Here it is hot	
sun and blue skies	random notes carefully played on chime bars or glockenspiel
birds	bells, recorder mouthpieces
gentle breeze	shakers, voices
the feel of heat	an occasional quiet strike on the cymbal, wobble a beater over two or three low notes on a glockenspiel or metallophone

Keep the first attempts very short. Encourage the children to listen to one another as they play and appoint a conductor to stop and start the players.

Each sound picture could finish with a peal of bells: just play down a glockenspiel, metallophone, or chime bars from top C to bottom C several times.

CHINESE NEW YEAR

Background information

The **Spring Festival** which marks the beginning of the Chinese Lunar New Year is the most important festival of the year for every Chinese family. It falls on a different day each year, usually late January or February, as its date is determined by the phases of the moon. The celebrations end fourteen days later with the **Lantern** (Yuanxiao) **Festival** which dates back more than 2,000 years.

The Spring Festival

Traditionally this is considered the time for clearing up, paying off debts and spring cleaning the house from top to bottom, in preparation for a prosperous year ahead. Flowers of prosperity decorate homes, offices and factories for this national holiday, a time when families make special efforts to get together. Special food is prepared, such as the dumplings that are traditional in various regions. Celebrations begin on the New Year's Eve with a 'New Year Unity Dinner', a large meal sometimes consisting of more than ten dishes. New Year's greetings, often written with a Chinese ink brush on red paper, are posted on the doors and greetings cards are exchanged. The evening ends late with firework displays, a special treat for the children.

In the morning of the New Year everyone puts on their new or best clothes to visit family and friends. Breakfast may consist of sweet or meat rice dumplings and rice cake. Children wish their parents a happy New Year and in return receive sweets. They may have already found little red packages of sweets or money under their pillows on waking! The traditional respect shown to parents

and elders is still part of their upbringing though the old custom of showing respect by a low bow known as 'kow towing' is gradually dying out.

Thus the Spring Festival is spent meeting relatives and friends and visiting museums, temples and places of entertainment. Some shops stay open and in places like Peking large open markets take place at that time. The familiar greeting 'Kung hei fat choy' means Happy New Year and recalls the five blessings of luck, food, long life, health and peace.

The Lantern Festival

At the end of two weeks the celebrations end with the Lantern Festival when, as you would expect, the main decorations are lanterns. These come in different shapes and sizes and hang everywhere both in and out doors. There is music and dancing in the streets. In Hong Kong a special feature of the festival is the dragon dance, relatively rare elsewhere because of the large space needed to accommodate the dancers, sometimes as many as twenty-two. An enormous dragon face and body, supported by a team of dancers, weaves its way through the streets to the music of a large drum, cymbals and tambourine. It will go to visit every house stopping to dance in the front yard when the dancers will usually receive a red packet containing money from the householders.

In London there are big celebrations every year in Soho. Here it is lions that parade and dance through the streets. Crowds gather to watch their antics as they try to reach for the chinese cabbages and envelopes of money that hang from many of the upper windows of shops and homes.

The children will be interested to learn that each

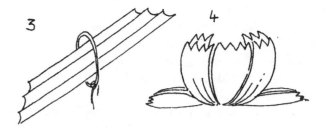

year in the Chinese calendar is named after an animal. One legend goes that the 12 animals chosen argued about who should be the first. So the gods decided to solve the matter by arranging a race across a big river; the winner was to be the first. The ox was winning but the clever rat jumped on his back to keep up then jumped off his back as he approached the bank and got there first. Thus the order of the years are:

first – rat   1972
second – ox   1973
third – tiger   1974
fourth – hare   1975
fifth – dragon   1976
sixth – snake   1977
seventh – horse   1978
eight – ram   1979
ninth – monkey   1980
tenth – cockerel   1981
eleventh – dog   1982
twelfth – pig   1983
first – rat   1984 (and so on)

The children might like to make a drawing of the animal of the year of their birth in the Chinese calendar and do the same for their brothers, sisters or friends.

Art and craft

Flowers of prosperity

1 Stack 8 to 10 pieces of tissue paper – shades of red, orange and pink. Trace pattern on top sheet and cut out the stack of tissues all at once.

2 Holding stack together, fold several times lengthwise like an accordion.

3 Twist string or coloured wool tightly around the middle.

4 Carefully pull up the petals one by one, arranging each one gently to form a flower. Decorate with shiny strips or glitter as required.

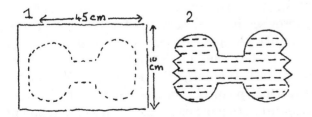

Dragons

A really large model will inspire the children to improvise their own dragon dance. You will need a large strong carton for the head, some long curtaining for the body and some sturdy sticks or broom handles of suitable length to support the entire creation. Individual heads will vary according to the creative ideas of the children. Assemble some good illustrations to get going. Another idea would be to use strong wire for the framework and to build the head with papier mâché or Polyfilla.

Mobile dragon
Use paper plates or pieces of cut, round card and hang from a stick or strong piece of string.

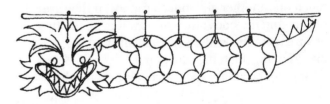

Baby dragon
Use cotton reels for the body and yoghurt or similar cartons for the head.

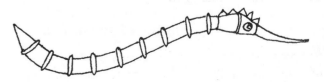

101

Paper flying dragon

The head – draw a head on both sides of a piece of folded paper about 8 cm long.

The body – Make two narrow strips about 60 cm long and 4 cm wide from coloured tissue, sugar paper or newspaper.

Glue the ends as shown, then keep folding across, (a) across (c), (b) across (c) until all the paper is folded into a concertina.

Glue the head and body together, place on a small cane or stick and run to make it fly.

Other ideas can include dragon masks and puppets.

Music and movement

Dragon drance

For the large street dragons the music is mainly improvised on large drums, cymbals and tambourines and follows closely the movements of the dancers. This would be suitable for a dragon dance in the hall with or without a dragon costume/ model.

Six or seven children can space out behind a leader as the body of the dragon. They need not touch one another and indeed cannot, if they are supporting the body; they must watch all the time to anticipate the leader's movements and the direction in which they are going.

In preparation for the dance it is best for the children to begin by working on their own. The speed should never be fast for obvious reasons! Here are some suggestions for ideas on which the children can base their movement, and for a percussive accompaniment:

Suggested percussion

stomping – steady not too heavy walk

 steady beat on a tambour or deep sounding drum

creeping – shuffling steps

 circular scraping movements on the tambour or drum head – scraping sou on a small cymbal

roaring – the dragon rears up

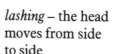 repeated beats on the tambour – clash on the big cymbal

lashing – the head moves from side to side

 crashes on the cymbal

playing – the dragon tries to get money envelopes hanging from windows

bells – very quiet drum

Drumming forms the traditional accompaniment to the dragon and lion dance. However, as this may not be sufficient to sustain the movement interest of younger children the above suggestions provide for a more varied dance. With some children it might be best to work out a sequence of movements. Others will prefer to improvise all the time so the musicians must be alert.

Lion heads are easier for smaller children and better for movement as they can be used on their own.

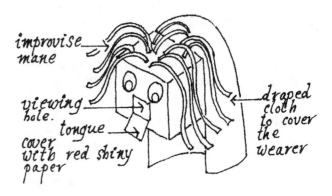

Lion dance

Music and movement for the lion dance will be improvised in the same way as for the dragon dance, but will underline the character of the lion. The walk will be proud, more feline; the head will turn from side to side and, of course, there will be the occasional 'pounce'. The characteristic rhythm to be heard during the dance in Gerrard Street, Soho, is usually played on the tambourine ♩ ♫♩ ♫.

Music for smaller (classroom) dragons

Use a small bongo drum, finger cymbals, bells and triangle. The children can work together in small groups with these instruments and any small models or puppets that they have made. Let them improvise movement and sound accompaniment and then work towards a more formal dance which will involve collective agreement on a music or movement pattern or even a narrative sequence:

Suggested percussion

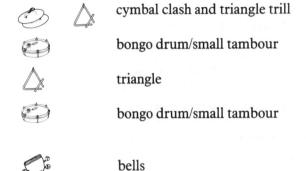

Enter the dragon in search of food	cymbal clash and triangle trill
The dragon stomps around	bongo drum/small tambour
He stops, lifts his head and sniffs	triangle
He stomps off again (Repeat last two movements for an agreed number of times)	bongo drum/small tambour
He plays with a Chinese cabbage	bells
He falls asleep	quiet triangle or finger cymbal

Lanterns

1 Take a piece of white paper A4 size (21 cm × 30 cm). Rule a margin 2 cm along the top and bottom with paper lengthwise. Let the children draw a colourful picture or pattern between the margins. Fold the paper in half lengthwise. Make straight cuts from the folded edge up to the margins. Colour the margins or stick on a length of bright shiny paper – red is a good colour. Open out and stick the edges to form the lantern. Improvise a handle.

Turning the paper the other way will give a different shaped latern. Use different coloured background paper. Spray with glitter for further effect.

2 Very simple lanterns can be made from thin card or sugar paper folded double for extra strength. A suitable size would be 42 cm × 16 cm. Fold in a strip about 2 cm from one end. Fold the rest in half lengthways, then fold the edges in so that they meet in the centre.

Stick strips of brightly coloured shiny paper down the sides and along the top and bottom edges. Decorate each 'face' with cut out symbolic shapes and back with coloured tissue paper. Decorations often include the name of the sender. Then stick the two edges to form the lantern and improvise a handle.

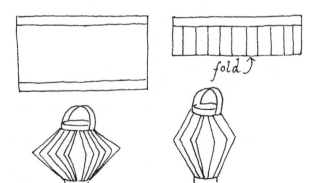

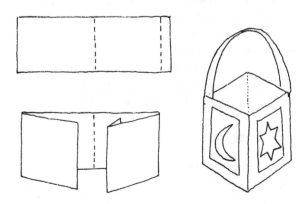

Miscellaneous

1 The children can practise writing with brushes and ink.
2 Try to collect some Chinese New Year cards to inspire ones that the children can make.
3 Assemble some Chinese objects like fans, shoes, china wear, books and lanterns so that the children and teacher can make a display for everyone to see.

Festival food

The kitchen becomes an important place at the time of the New Year festival for in some homes the family will gather there to worship Tsao-Shen (the God of the kitchen or 'furnace'). During the week before the festival this god is believed to go up to heaven and report on the conduct of each member of the family during the past year. On New Year's Eve the god will return and the evening is celebrated with a special meal.

The traditional food is dumpling. 'We like it not only because it is very delicious, but because of its method of preparation. It is more important than eating them. Always the whole family sits together and talks to each other and makes dumplings together. It is full of family affection.' *Shi Likai (Peking)* from *Chinese New Year, Something to Celebrate* pack, Bedford Resources Unit.

The type of dumpling varies according to the tradition of each region. **Chiaotzu** are made from wheat flour and water. The dough is rolled out into long rolls from which sections are cut and flattened into rounds of about 6 cm. These 'wrappers' are then filled with chopped pork, cabbage and spring onion, flavoured with ginger, soya sauce, salt, pepper and sesame oil, sealed and boiled in water until done. They are served with vinegar and soya sauce. Some parents might like to try making them at home; they would not be easy to make at school with young children.

The following recipe will involve the children in making the little biscuit-type 'cruller', but the cooking in oil *must* be done by an adult.

New Year Cruller

250g (10 oz) plain flour
75g (3 oz) sugar
75g (3 oz) lard

2 eggs
1 tablespoon water (as necessary)

METHOD
1 Sift flour on to a table and make a hollow in the centre.
2 Put sugar, lard, beaten eggs into the hollow and work into a soft dough. Add water if necessary.
3 Sift a little flour on to the table and roll out to a thickness of ½ cm. Cut out shapes with biscuit cutters.
4 Heat pan with oil. Put in the biscuits when the oil is ready to boil. Deep fry over low heat until golden brown. Take out and drain on kitchen paper. Keep in an airtight plastic box.

Fried mixed vegetables

100g (4 oz) mushrooms
½ a cucumber
1 carrot
1 stick of celery
50g (2 oz) bamboo shoots
1 can bean sprouts
3 tablespoons peanut oil
1 tablespoon soy sauce
½ level teaspoon sugar
150ml (¼ pint) water
2 level teaspoons cornflour

METHOD
1 Cut and slice finely mushrooms, cucumber, carrot, celery, bamboo shoots and bean sprouts.
2 Heat peanut oil in a heavy frying pan and add the sliced vegetables. Fry gently, stirring all the time, for three to five minutes.
3 Mix together the sugar, soy sauce and cornflour; gradually add the water to make a smooth paste.
4 Add to the vegetables and boil for one minute.
5 Serve immediately.

This easy vegetable recipe will demonstrate to the children the 'secret' of the art of Chinese cookery: the fact that most of the time is taken up in careful preparation and that the cooking time is very short. Vegetables are usually cooked without water, so that their colour remains fresh and vitamin content is not lost. Prepare this dish just before lunch time if you can; borrow some chopsticks and try them out.

Better still would be to invite some parents into school to help the children cook a complete meal.

Merry have we met

Gaily

Mer - ry have we met and mer - ry we re - main;

Mer - ry let us part and mer - ry meet a - gain.

Mer - ry mer - ry sing song, hap - py, gay and free,

With a mer - ry ding dong a - gain we'll hap - py be.

This simple Chinese tune is based on the following group of notes which is the pentatonic scale on F:

F G A C' D'

It can be accompanied by any of these notes grouped to fit rhythms based on words from the song. Here are some suggestions:

Suggested instruments

chime bars or recorder

Ding dong

xylophone

Mer - ry have we met

glockenspiel

Mer - ry sing song

A little ensemble could be built up with the tune played on the piano by a beginner pianist, on the recorder by an older child or on the glockenspiel by anyone who can manage it (or on two or all of these instruments).

Playing by ear

Sing the first line to the children, showing them by moving your hand in the air how the tune goes up and then down. Let them join in. Now show them how to play the first part on the chime bars. Prepare a simple work card for practice in the music corner:

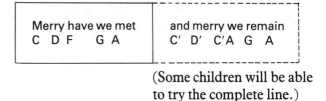

Merry have we met	and merry we remain
C D F G A	C' D' C' A G A

(Some children will be able to try the complete line.)

The first and third lines are exactly the same. Sing through quietly and ask the children to tell you when they hear the tune of the first line coming again.

Chinese New Year

Chinese song

Not too fast

I'm a lit-tle Chi-nese girl --------- is my name,
(boy)

This is what I al-ways do On Chi-nese New Year day.

Kow Tow first to Pa-pa, Ma-ma, Then to un-cles aun-ties too,

How I love the Chi-nese New Year, Eve-ry one does too!

This simple action song is suitable for younger children. It is based on the **pentatonic** (or **five note**) scale which gives the 'sound' of Chinese tunes. 'Kow tow' means a low bow and was the way people in China showed their respect for their elders. Although the custom of kow towing is rapidly dying out in modern China, many families, especially those who keep to the more traditional way of life, observe this custom at festival time.

Divide the children into families and let them all have a turn at being the elders. These characters will sit sedately on chairs while the 'children' take turns at paying their respects. The children can choose Chinese names for themselves and one or two may even be able to sing by themselves.

Suggested percussion

Quiet percussion can accompany lines 3 and 4. Finger cymbals or Indian bells would be suitable. Several children could play and could work out their own way of accompanying.

Playing by ear

The first line uses four notes only – D E G A. Show the children how to play the first two bars 'I'm a little Chinese girl', then see if they can work out the next two which end on the lower note D. Leave these chime bars in the music corner together with a simple work card:

I'm a little Chinese girl
G A G A E E E

Chinese New Year

Low Siew Poh

Merrily

1 Chi-nese New Year is here a - gain, Here a - gain, here a - gain,

Chi-nese New Year is here a - gain, Let us now re - joice._____

2 Down in the streets crackers sound,
Crackers sound, crackers sound,
Down in the streets crackers sound,
Bing, bing, bang bang Bong.

3 Children darting here and there,
Here and there, here and there,
Children darting here and there,
Hee, hee, ha, ha, ha.

4 Look over there I see a lion,
See a lion, see a lion,
Look over there I see a lion,
Prancing up and down.

5 In every house the elders shout,
Elders shout, elders shout,
In every house the elders shout,
Yam Seng.

6 Children all get red packets,
Red packets, red packets,
Children all get red packets,
From every one.

7 When friends meet they all will greet,
All will greet, all will greet,
When friends meet they all will greet,
Kong Hee Fatt Choy.

8 Let us all then celebrate,
Celebrate, celebrate,
Let us all then celebrate,
Happy New Year.

Suggested percussion

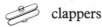 clappers

finger cymbals

 drum

(none)

 triangle

 tambourine

 all

Singing game

Sing and mime in a circle as in 'Here we go round
the mulberry bush'.

Playing by ear

This melody very clearly goes up and down the six
notes C D E G A C' which is the
pentatonic group on C. Leave these chime bars in

the music corner so that the children can practise
playing up and down. Encourage them to use the
rhythm of the song and provide a simple work card
to help them start:

> Chinese New Year is here again
> C D E G A C' A G

Boat song

Chinese children's song (Hokkien dialect).
English words and arrangement by Gaik See Choo

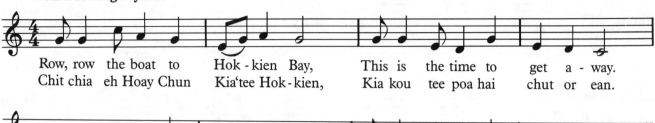

With a rowing rhythm

Row, row the boat to Hok-kien Bay, This is the time to get a-way.
Chit chia eh Hoay Chun Kia'tee Hok-kien, Kia kou tee poa hai chut or ean.

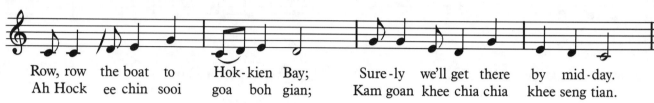

Row, row the boat to Hok-kien Bay; Sure-ly we'll get there by mid-day.
Ah Hock ee chin sooi goa boh gian; Kam goan khee chia chia khee seng tian.

Suggested percussion

large cymbal with wire brush

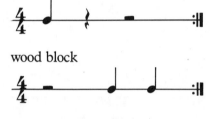

wood block

bass or alto xylophone

C chord   G chord

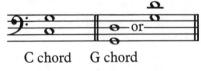

C C C C   C C G G   G G G G   G G C C

C C C C   C C G G   G G G G   G G C C

Two children, one to each chord, can accompany throughout on the beat. Teachers could use a guitar to quietly support this accompaniment.

Teachers wishing to add further percussion can base ostinato (repeat) patterns on some of the word rhythms:

Suggested percussion

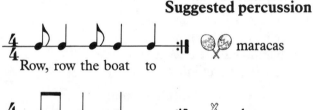

Row, row the boat to — maracas

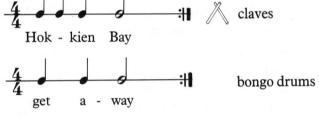

Hok - kien Bay — claves

get a - way — bongo drums

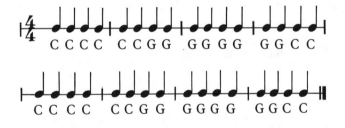

Recorder

An older child could play the tune on a recorder (or glockenspiel).

Movement

Use this song unaccompanied with younger children and let them enjoy the rowing movements as they sing.

Lantern song

Chinese song arranged by Kenneth Pont,
adapted by Jean Gilbert

Leisurely

RECORDERS

VOICES

Let's go and see the

INDIAN BELLS

lan - terns to - day   lan - terns __ in   the   first ___ month,
second ___ month,
third ___ month,

RECORDERS

lan - terns through the __ streets.

VOICES

RECORDERS

What are the lan - terns we can see?

VOICES

Bar 16

We   can see the   hea - ven cloud   lan - terns burn - ing   bright.
dra - gon flow'r
three - fold star

Suggested accompaniments

1 Indian bells (or finger cymbals)

come and see   come and see

This part is indicated in the song. Alternatively,
younger children could maintain the beat

throughout or just during the recorder part. The
recorder part could be played on a melodic
instrument or hummed by a small group.

2 Chime bars, glockenspiel or metallophone

Bars 1–16   Last two bars

109

Feng Yang Song

Chinese folk song arranged by Evelyn Chua

Lively

Left hand holds the drum, right hand holds the drum. Both hands will play the drum

as we sing our song. We love to sing songs, __ come and sing __ too.

Bar 8   Bar 9

We love to sing and play on our fest - ive day. Feng Yang __ Feng Yang, __

Ye __ ya, __ ya ye ya; Troo, ling ling ling ling ling, Troo, ling ling ling ling ling,

Troo ling ling, Troo ling ling, Troo ling ling ling ling ling ling ling ling ling ling ling.

'Feng Yang' is pronounced 'Fung Yang'. The 'r' should be rolled when singing the word 'Troo'.

There are many versions of this traditional folk song. I heard this one being taught in Argyle Junior School in London by Evelyn Chua who translated and adapted the words. She remembers the song as a great favourite during festival celebrations.

Descant recorders could introduce the song by playing the first four bars. They would give the nearest sound to the Chinese flute which is a popular traditional instrument.

Suggested percussion

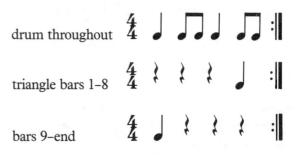

drum throughout

triangle bars 1–8

bars 9–end

This accompaniment could be simplified by playing the *first* and *third* beats in the bar – mainly all Cs.

xylophone

More songs from China and about China

There are very few songs specifically to do with the Chinese New Year; they are mostly to do with aspects of China and its history or traditional folk songs.

The Lantern Song Book
Collected and arranged by Kenneth Pont (O.U.P.)

This collection contains simple arrangements of ten Chinese songs for voices, recorders and percussion. Mainly for older children but some of the simpler melodies would appeal to younger children:

Come, let's pick some tea, Mm –
Sing this song with me, Mm –
Fill the baskets to the brim with the
fresh green leaves of tea.
            (Tea Pickers' Song)

Pentatonic Song Book
Edited and arranged by Brian Brocklehurst (Schott)

There are five Chinese songs in this collection. Younger children would enjoy:

'Chimes at night'
'Fengyang Drum' (another version of the song in this section)

All Asia sings
World Around Songs series (Informal Music Service, Delaware, Ohio, U.S.A.)

The Yangtze Boatmen's Chantey reminds us of a very common theme in folk music. There are nine other songs of varying appeal in this little volume.

'My ship sailed from China'
from *Apusskidu* (A. & C. Black)

'Chinatown dragon'
from *Harlequin* (A. & C. Black)

Both the above songs are relevant but have western melodies.

'Ming-Ming and the Lantern Dragon'
by Douglas Coombes and John E. Edwards from *Time and Tune* (B.B.C.)

This is a musical play with songs and activities. Ming-Ming, a young village boy, works out how to scare away Kong-Sang, the Sun Dragon, and ends a drought that has devastated the land.

Poems

Don't ask me why

Mamma gave me two cakes.
I hid one in a secret place.
Don't ask me why.

Daddy made me wear winter clothes.
I won't wear them.
Don't ask me why.

My brother gave me some song-sheets.
I chose the nicest one.
Don't ask me why.

I put them all by my bed at night.
And, under my quilt, let my dreams fly.
Don't ask me why.

I'll ask a girl to eat the cake,
And give her the clothes for the winter snow.
Together we'll sing the nicest song.

If you want to know who she is,
Go and ask Grandpa Andersen –
She's the little girl who sells matches.

Liu Qianqian (aged nine)

Liu Qianqian refers to the little match girl in the
story by Hans Andersen. He believed that she
would not have died of hunger if she had lived in his
city.

To welcome the bright tomorrow

I had a dream,
I walked into a garden.
There were many children
Working there.
I saw some white children,
I saw some black children,
I saw some golden-haired children
I saw some blue-eyed children,
Watering flowers and planting trees, you helped me,
Pulling weeds and catching worms, I helped you.
A black boy came in an airship,
And, removing many stars from the sky,
Hung them up on the trees
To make lanterns for our garden.
We were singing and dancing
In the Spring breezes of the garden . . .
I told Mamma the dream after I woke up.
Mamma said, 'That is not a dream,
Tomorrow it will come true –
Happiness and peace.'

Tian Xiafel (aged nine)

These two poems won national prizes in late 1980 in an international competition of children's poetry sponsored by the United Nations Educational, Scientific and Cultural Organization. (UNESCO) The theme of the contest was 'Children helping one another'.

Quiet night thoughts

Before my bed
there is bright moonlight
So that it seems
like frost on the ground:

Lifting my head
I watch the bright moon,
Lowering my head
I dream that I'm home.

Li Po

Wandering breezes

The catkins line the lanes,
making white carpets,
And leaves on lotus streams
spread like green money:

Pheasants root bamboo shoots,
nobody looking,
While ducklings on the sands
sleep by their mothers.

Tu Fu

Li Po (A.D. 701–62) and Tu Fu (A.D. 712–70) are generally regarded by the Chinese to be two of their greatest poets, and the age in which they lived has been thought of as '. . . the most golden of all the golden ages of Chinese poetry;'

Background information

Holi is a Hindu spring festival coinciding with the month of March when, in India, the main crops are almost ripe for the spring harvest and when the spring flowers are blossoming. The festival lasts for five days and is known as the festival of colour. It is a great social occasion, a time for visiting friends, for exchanging gifts of savouries and sweetmeats and a season of goodwill all round.

Holi usually begins with the lighting of fires. A big bonfire centrally placed is lit by a Brahman priest; this is the signal for the lighting of any other bonfires that have been made ready in the area. A popular ritual with the children is the burning of a made-up figure of Holika, a legendary character, on the communal bonfire. This is often followed by the burning of rubbish and various articles to symbolize the forgiveness of past misdeeds and the triumph of good over evil.

After the bonfires comes the 'throwing of colour'. People buy coloured dust which they throw about with water and balloons; they regard it as lucky to be sprinkled in this way. They join in with dancing and revelry and follow processions which may include enormous floats carrying statues of the gods.

Tie-dyeing

This is a suitable activity to associate with the Holi festival as it encourages the children to think about colour. Start with something simple such as children's scarves and table cloths cut from discarded white sheeting, or plain white Tee shirts.

The fabric is first knotted; it can be tied around pebbles or other round objects with string, or twisted around a stick and tied up with string. It is then placed in a dye bath for about five minutes, taken out, rinsed and dried. If another colour is going to be used as well, the procedure is the same but the knots can be tied in different places. There are different kinds of dyes on the market, so follow the instructions for the one being used.

When mixing colours, begin with the light colours and consider the way the colours mix. Pink and mauve, for instance, will give you a pink, blue and mauve design; yellow and blue will give a yellow, blue and green design.

Let the children mix paints for the colours they have chosen for tie-dyeing and try to forecast the colour design they hope to achieve.

Art and craft and festival food

See suggestions in the Diwali section.

Stick dance Kolattam

Indian folk dance collected by Janet E. Tobitt,
Words adapted by Jean Gilbert

1 Come mai - dens fair al - to - ge - ther come.
  (boys and girls)

Danc - ing in a ring - o, round and round and round we go.

CHORUS

Love - ly co - lours, see them all,

Danc - ing light - ly, clap - ping gai - ly, joy - ful - ly we sing.

2 Reverence to elders we must show. (repeat)
  Best of daughters (children) we will always be. (repeat)
  CHORUS

3 Lightly we step with bells upon our feet, (repeat)
  Holding rainbow coloured sticks as we go dancing round. (repeat)
  CHORUS

4 Now here's the end. Our song and dance are done. (repeat)
  We have tried to do our best to please you all and everyone. (repeat)
  CHORUS

This is a girls' dance but it can be adapted as
suggested to include the boys. The dancers sing at
the same time; however, younger children will find
this difficult as the words are non-repetitive, so
there could be a separate group to do the singing.
The sticks can be brightly painted and ribboned
and the dancers can wear bells sewn on elastic
around their ankles.

There must be an even number of dancers so that
a double circle can be formed with partners facing
one another. Children in the inner circle kneel on
left knees; those in the outer circle stand and keep
step throughout the song by tapping alternate toes
on the ground.

Line 1
Partners strike each other's right-hand sticks, then
left-hand sticks:

right hand strikes   left hand strikes

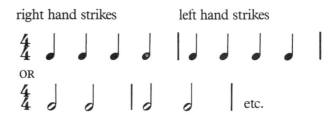

OR

etc.

Line 1 (repeat)
Partners strike both sticks and the standing circle
moves one place to the left to find a new partner:

both hands strike   move to the left

This pattern is continued until original partners
meet. Then the inner circle stands while the outer
circle kneels and the dance is repeated.

115

Holi festival of colour

Punitha Perinparaja

A *Rhythmically*

Throw .the wa - ters, co - loured wa - ters, Ho - li Fes - ti - val's here.____

B

Mu - si - cians play - ing, drum-mers beat - ing, Pro-ces - sions lead - ing through the streets.

C

Joy - ful - ly child - ren dance and sing, Ho - li the col-lour-ful Fes - ti - val of Spring.

D

Friends and re - la - tions all __ will meet, Sweet-meats, bal-loons for when they greet.

E

Throw_the wa - ters, co - loured wa - ters, Ho - li Fes - ti - val's here.____

Note The raga on which this song is based is the authentic equivalent of a major scale, the scale of C as written. Improvisations based on this raga C D E F G A B C' can introduce the dance.

The dancers can be accompanied by a group of singers. If the dance is performed without the song, the tune can be played by a recorder, or by a beginner pianist.

Dance

A1 } The children take partners in line formation.
A2 } They enter, walking rhythmically and clapping two light sticks (decorated with ribbons). The pattern is two claps above heads – straight elbows – and two claps low down:

(high) (low) (high) (low)

The children face their partners in two lines ready for the next section.

B1 Both lines kneel and clap their own sticks in this pattern:

clap, twirl right stick clap, twirl left stick

B2 Stand up and do the same movements.

C1 Facing partners, clap own stick, clap partner's right stick; clap own stick, clap partner's left stick; change places clapping own sticks.

C2 Repeat

D1 Repeat B2 movements (standing up).

D2 Repeat B2 movements turning round on the spot.

E1 ⎤ The children go off in a line repeating the
E2 ⎦ A movements.

At some point during the dance two children can throw 'coloured water' over the dancers. This could be tiny round pieces of multi-coloured tissue paper, rather like confetti.

Suggestions for accompaniments

Introduction for piano, recorders and glocks:

bass xylophone

The piano (or any other tuned instrument) now plays the melody and drone (low C as for bass xylophone) throughout.

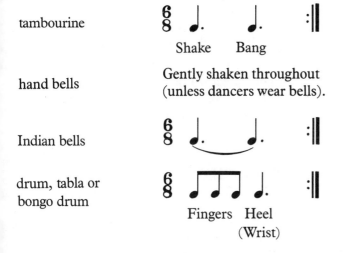

tambourine

Shake   Bang

hand bells — Gently shaken throughout (unless dancers wear bells).

Indian bells

drum, tabla or bongo drum

Fingers   Heel
(Wrist)

PESACH

Background information

Pesach or Passover is the Jewish festival of freedom. It lasts for eight days and usually takes place in April at about the same time as Easter. It recalls the story of the Exodus from Egypt where the Israelites had been enslaved for 210 years, and celebrates their passing over from slavery to freedom. Pharaoh, the Egyptian ruler, finally let them go after the ten plagues, attributed to the Jewish God, had ravaged the land and its people. They were led out of Egypt by Moses to wander for many years through the wilderness before reaching the promised land now known as Israel.

In their hasty departure the Jews baked only unleavened bread; there was no leaven to make the dough rise and they hadn't any time for preparation. And ever since then at the time of Passover, **matza**, which is unleavened and looks like a flat cracker biscuit, is eaten instead of bread. No food is allowed that has had any contact with risen flour or yeast, so a thorough spring clean goes on before Passover. Orthodox households will have a complete set of cooking dishes for special use during this festival; these are often handed down from mother to daughter.

A family ceremony known as a **seder** (pronounced say-da) service is held on the first two nights of the festival. When everyone is gathered round the table, the youngest child asks four questions starting with 'why is this night so different from all other nights?' The head of the family then relates the story of the Exodus from Egypt, reading and singing from the **Haggadah**; this is the order of the service and contains an ancient explanation and comments on its significance. The service is interrupted by a festival meal and concludes with the singing of hymns and popular folk songs.

Symbols form an important part of the evening. The table will include:

a roasted shank bone of a lamb to commemorate the sacrifice that was made in olden times

bitter herbs (more accurately bitter vegetables), usually horseradish, as a reminder of the harshness of slavery

charoset (haroset), a mixture of chopped nuts, apples and wine to represent the mortar used by the Jews in their forced labour

karpas, a green plant like parsley, as a symbol of springtime and hope

salt water for tears shed by the slaves and the crossing of the Red Sea

a roast or 'burnt' egg as a festival offering

a plate of matzos recalling the hasty flight from Egypt

Four cups of wine must be drunk as a reminder of the four promises made by God to redeem Israel. This is a happy, family occasion and an important time for the children who symbolize the future.

Art and craft

Paint or draw scenes to illustrate the story of the Exodus, referring to suitable pictorial references to ancient Egyptian art. These could include life as a slave under Egyptian rule, some of the ten plagues, crossing the Red Sea and the wanderings in the wilderness.

Paint and decorate paper plates with Pesach symbols:

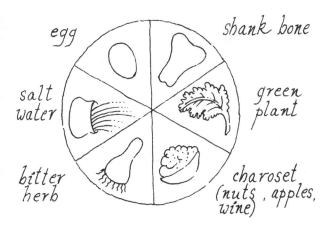

One or two coats of clear varnish will give a professional finish.

This activity will be more meaningful if the children can have the opportunity to see and talk about these things. Bring a lamb bone in to school or visit a local butchers. Make up a small bowl of charoset. If you have some Jewish children in your group perhaps they and their parents could show how the table is laid for Pesach and talk about how they celebrate this festival.

Recipe for charoset

1 small apple peeled and cored
a few dates, stoned
a few seedless raisins
1 teaspoon candied peel
a few peeled almonds
cinnamon to taste

Chop or mince ingredients very finely, add cinnamon and moisten with a little wine (or apple juice).

Festival food

During the Passover festival, it is forbidden to eat or use any flour, cereals, dried peas, beans, yeast, baking powder and anything that may have had contact with leaven or raising agents. Cooking stoves and fridges are thoroughly cleaned and cooking utensils, cutlery and crockery are changed in every orthodox Jewish family. Only recipes that do not contain any of the prohibited ingredients are allowed and sometimes potato flour or fine matzo meal may be substituted.

'The feast of unleavened bread shalt thou keep. Seven days thou shalt eat unleavened bread, as I commanded thee . . .'   *Exodus* 34 v. 18

If you can invest in a large packet of matzos and some matzo meal there are a number of ways the children can savour this aspect of the festival food apart from just eating the crispy biscuits on their own or with butter or margarine and a sweet or savoury topping. Soak them first until they are soft but not soggy, dip them in beaten egg and fry until crisp and brown. Break them up for this. Soak until very soft, squeeze out and add to a scrambled egg mixture.

Matzo pudding

Cook this in the morning with a small group. Share it around at lunch time.

3 matzos
100g (4 oz) fine matzo meal
50g (2 oz) ground almonds
100g (4 oz) sultanas
50g (2 oz) currants
100 (4 oz) sugar
2 eggs
1 teaspoon cinnamon or mixed spice
grated rind and juice of one lemon
1 tablespoon margarine or fat for baking

METHOD
1 Soak matzos until soft. Squeeze very dry and put in mixing bowl.
2 Add everything else (except fat) and mix thoroughly.
3 Melt fat in a baking dish and add the mixture.
4 Bake in a moderate oven for about one hour.

Enlist the help of Jewish parents or those with a knowledge of Jewish food if you can. They will add authority to this aspect of your festival topic and perhaps some more recipes to try.

119

We were slaves   Ava-dim Hayinou

Music by Shalom Postolsky,
words from the Haggadah translated by Eve Benjamin.
English lyrics by Jean Gilbert.

With feeling

We were slaves in E - gypt ___ long a - go, Yes we were slaves in E - gypt so
A - va - dim Ha - yi - nou ___ A - va dim A - ta be - nei cho - rin ___ Be -

long a - go. Now we're free, ___ We are free, ___ But
- nie cho - rin. A - va - dim ___ Ha - yi - nou. A -

we were slaves in E - gypt's land. ___ Now we're free,
ta a - ta be - nei cho - rin. ___ A - va - dim

We are free, but we were slaves in E - gypt's land so long a - go.
Ha - yi - nou a - ta a - ta be nei cho - rin be - nei cho - rin.

The words on which the translated setting is based come from the story of the Exodus written in the Haggadah.

The song is more suitable for older children and could well support any drama connected with this epic story. The singing should be clear, firm and unhurried.

Suggested percussion

This can underline the two statements, one about slavery, the other about the supreme joy of freedom. It should be played with some restraint for the words should speak for themselves.

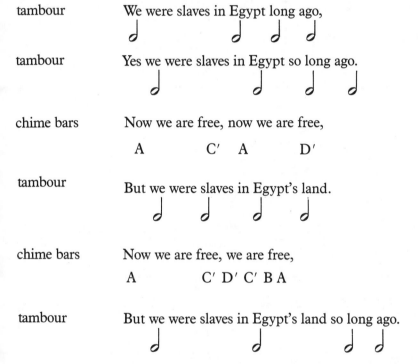

tambour   We were slaves in Egypt long ago,

tambour   Yes we were slaves in Egypt so long ago.

chime bars   Now we are free, now we are free,

       A   C′ A   D′

tambour   But we were slaves in Egypt's land.

chime bars   Now we are free, we are free,

       A   C′ D′ C′ B A

tambour   But we were slaves in Egypt's land so long ago.

A background talk about slavery would underline the full meaning of this song.

Dayenu

Hebrew melody, words from the Passover Haggadah

A literal translation is as follows:

If He had done nothing more than take us out of Egypt,
For that alone, we should have been grateful.

The refrain of 'Dayenu' means 'For that alone, we should have been grateful'.

As a rhythm clapping game the song can be divided into two parts:

A

Use the whole section for clapping.
Nursery children can clap the beat throughout.
Young children can clap their own hands and then their partners, sitting or standing freely.
Older children can sit or stand facing their partner in a line and try this more complicated clapping

pattern: one line claps *on* the beat, while the other line claps *in between* the beats.
e.g. Children in one line clap

Children facing them clap

They do this for the first two bars then clap the last two bars of section A together.

(long   long   short short long)

B

This part is a dance.
Nursery and younger children can skip freely on their own or with a partner.
Older children can make up a more formal dance pattern or even try to dance a polka – one, two, three, hop, etc.

Everyone is then ready to start all over again.

Suggested accompaniment

Optional percussion:

Section A

Keep the beat going with a wood block or clappers.
Older children would accompany the more complicated clapping game with two different instruments, say a wood block and a tambourine, one playing on the beat, the other playing on the off beat.

Section B

Younger children could play on the beat with a tambourine.
Older children could use the tambourine to underline the polka step:

etc.

Wherefore is it different?　Ma Nishtana

Israeli folk melody.
Words from the Haggadah

124

The Seder

The words of the four prescribed questions asked during the Seder service are set to this beautiful folk melody. It can be heard in Israel in school during the weeks preceding Pesach and in every home on the first night of Pesach. The words of the first verse are given above in Hebrew. As they do not sound well in English it is suggested that the children might like to try the original language. The phonetic sound is as written. A literal translation is given of all four questions:

1 Wherefore is this night different
  From all other nights?
  That on all other nights we eat
  Either leavened or unleavened bread,
  While on this night it must be unleavened bread.

2 Wherefore is this night different
  From all other nights?
  That on all other nights we eat
  Any species of herbs,
  While on this night we eat bitter herbs.

3 Wherefore is this night different
  From all other nights?
  That on all other nights we do not immerse
      the herbs[1] we eat
  Even once.
  While on this night we do it twice.

4 Wherefore is this night different
  From all other nights?
  That on all other nights we eat
  Either sitting or leaning,[2]
  While on this night we all lean.

[1] Parsley is dipped in salt water and the bitter herbs in charoset.
[2] Leaning against the table is a sign of freedom.

Fair is the twilight
And fragrant and still;
Little by little
The synagogues fill.

One by one kindle
The night's gleaming eyes;
Candles in windows
And stars in the skies.

Ended in school is
The service divine;
Seder is started
With legends and wine.

Father is blessing
The night of all nights;
All who are hungry
To feast he invites.

All who are homeless
Yet masters shall be,
Slaves who are this year –
The next shall be free!

Children ask 'questions',
And father replies;
Playfully sparkle
The wine and the eyes.

Songs of redemption
All merrily sing;
Queen is each mother,
Each father a king.

Midnight. The Seder
Is come to an end;
Guardian angels
From Heaven descend.

Each one a message
Of liberty brings;
Scattering blessings
Of peace from his wings.

Philip M. Raskin

One only kid (Had Gadya)

One only kid, one only kid,
My father bought for two zuzim.
One only kid, one only kid.

Then came a cat and ate the kid
My father bought for two zuzim.
One only kid, one only kid.

Then came a dog and bit the cat,
That ate the kid
My father bought for two zuzim.
One only kid, one only kid.

Then came a stick and beat the dog,
That bit the cat that ate the kid
My father bought for two zuzim.
One only kid, one only kid.

Then came a fire and burnt the stick,
That beat the dog that bit the cat
That ate the kid
My father bought for two zuzim.
One only kid, one only kid.

Then came the water and quenched the fire,
That burnt the stick that beat the dog
That bit the cat that ate the kid
My father bought for two zuzim.
One only kid, one only kid.

Then came an ox and drank the water,
That quenched the fire that burnt the stick
That beat the dog that bit the cat
That ate the kid
My father bought for two zuzim.
One only kid, one only kid.

Then came a butcher and slaughtered the ox,
That drank the water that quenched the fire
That burnt the stick that beat the dog
That bit the cat that ate the kid
My father bought for two zuzim.
One only kid, one only kid.

Then came the angel of death and killed the butcher,
That slaughtered the ox that drank the water
That quenched the fire that burnt the stick
That beat the dog that bit the cat
That ate the kid
My father bought for two zuzim.
One only kid, one only kid.

Then came the Holy One, blessed be He,
And slew the angel of death,
That killed the butcher that slaughtered the ox
That drank the water that quenched the fire
That burnt the stick that beat the dog
That bit the cat that ate the kid
My father bought for two zuzim.
One only kid, one only kid.

This poem comes at the end of the Passover Haggadah. It is a translation from the Aramaic. The word 'only' can be replaced by 'little' to give the repeat phrase 'One little kid, one little kid', if this is preferred.

Go down, Moses

Spiritual

1 When Is-rael was in E-gypt land, Let my peo-ple go; Op-

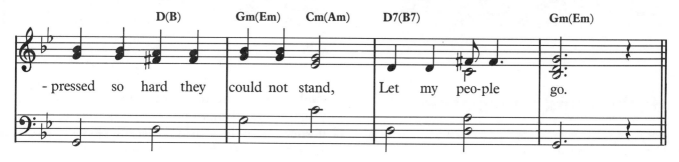

-pressed so hard they could not stand, Let my peo-ple go.

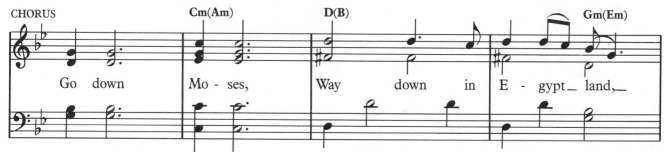

Go down Mo-ses, Way down in E-gypt_ land,_

Tell_ ol'_____ Pha-raoh to let my peo-ple go.

2 Thus spoke the Lord, bold Moses said,
Let my people go;
If not I'll smite your first born dead,
Let my people go.
CHORUS

3 No more shall they in bondage toil,
Let my people go;
Let them come out with Egypt's spoil,
Let my people go.
CHORUS

This song, which is more suitable for older
children, should be sung firmly, not too slowly, and
with great attention to the words.

Guitar
Guitar is easier in Em. Capo up 3 frets to sing in
Gm, or stay in Em if this is better for the children's
voices.

EASTER IN CYPRUS

Background information

Cyprus is a beautiful island, part of a great civilization and with an ancient history, rich in tradition which has changed very little over the centuries. Some of these traditions are reflected in the celebrations at Easter which is the major Christian festival among Greek Cypriots.

On Palm Sunday, worshippers take olive branches with them to church. They wave these as they process behind the priest to symbolize the welcome given to Jesus when he entered Jerusalem. The olive branches are left in the church for forty days for blessing, then they are collected and taken home. Here they are lit, put into a special pot to smoulder and are taken round the house so that all hatred shall be banished.

During Holy Week the sufferings of Jesus are remembered. The icons in church are covered with a black cloth while the villagers fast and attend services every evening. On Holy Thursday, the night of the crucifixion, single girls prepare garlands to hang by the cross and on their return home, drink some vinegar.

Church bells toll for the death of Jesus on Good Friday; young girls decorate the epitaph and in the evening groups of boys and girls dressed in white sing songs about Mary's bitterness over the unjust death of Jesus. The epitaph is processed through the streets in the evening and is returned to church where the older women remain to guard it overnight.

Saturday is the day for baking cakes, preparing plaited bread with sesame seed and dyeing eggs. It is also the day for the slaughtering of the pascal lamb ready for the main meal. The big service takes place on Sunday morning. The black cloth is dropped from the icon as the words 'God is risen' are sung, then the bells change their ringing. The priest brings out three lighted candles and from these householders light their own candles to 'bring new light into the home'. In the afternoon a big bonfire is lit on which is burnt the effigy of Judas. This is followed by firework displays while at home people eat their cakes and **flaounes** (see recipe) and play games with hard-boiled eggs. There is a further service on Sunday before the main meal of the festival. The lamb is barbecued and eaten with stuffed vine leaves, roast potatoes or macaroni moussaka, followed by fresh oranges and home-made cakes.

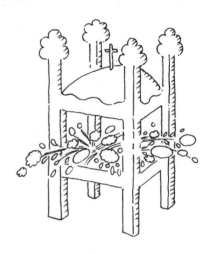

The **epitaph** (*epitaphios*) consists of a carved structure holding an embroidered icon of Jesus in the sepulchre. It is covered by rosemary which in turn is part of a decorative covering of thousands of fragrant flowers.

Festival food

Easter cakes (Flaounes)

These are very popular on Easter Saturday after the bonfire and firework displays. This recipe is from Nitsa Sergides.

THE FILLING
(prepare the day before)
300g (12 oz) unsalted Greek cheese or mild Cheddar
  cheese
4 eggs
50g (2 oz) fresh yeast
¼ teaspoon ground cinnamon
1 teaspoon baking powder
Fresh mint, about 3 stalks
¼ teaspoon mastihi (a kind of gum available from
  Greek shops)
¼ teaspoon mehlibi (small seeds available from
  Greek shops)

THE PASTRY
400g (1 lb) self-raising white flour
50g (2 oz) fat (Spry or Cookeen)
50g (2 oz) fresh yeast
¼ teaspoon cinnamon
¼ teaspoon mastihi
¼ teaspoon mehlibi
pinch salt
1 large glass warm water
1 tablespoon warm milk

THE SESAME SEEDS
Boil 150g (6 oz) sesame seeds for about ½ hour.
Rinse out water and dry on a tray.

Makes about 22 small cakes.

THE FILLING

1 Grind cheese into a bowl.

2 Dilute yeast with water. Add to cheese.

3 Cut mint into tiny pieces. Add to cheese. herbs baking powder

4 Breaks eggs into mixture. Bind together. *Leave overnight.*

THE PASTRY

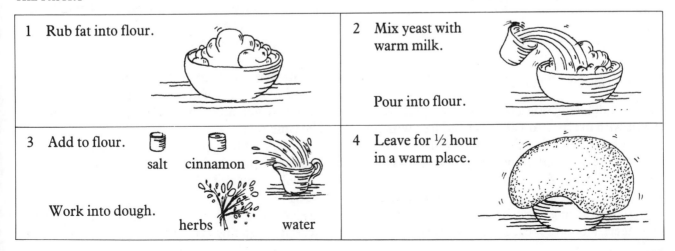

1 Rub fat into flour.

2 Mix yeast with warm milk. Pour into flour.

3 Add to flour. salt cinnamon Work into dough. herbs water

4 Leave for ½ hour in a warm place.

METHOD

1 Flatten and roll small pieces of dough into round pancakes. 	2 Press one side into tray of sesame seeds. 
3 Put few teaspoons filling onto other side.	4 Fold sides to make an open parcel. Press down corners with fork. 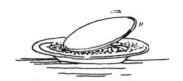
5 Brush top with beaten egg. 	6 Leave for ½ hour in warm place. 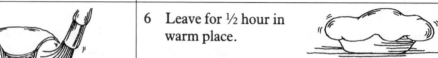 Cook in hot oven Regulo 6–7 (400°F/204°C) for about ½ hour until golden brown.

Children's games

Children enjoy these games on Easter Saturday and Sunday afternoons and evenings. They have been remembered by Nitsa Sergides.

Loudro

The children sit in a circle. One of them, Maria, stands up and touches another, Andrea, on the back. Immediately Andrea stands up and chases Maria who races round the outside of the sitting circle. She taps Maria on the shoulder when she catches her but Maria can tap Andrea's shoulder if she does not escape quickly enough. This continues until Maria admits defeat. She then chooses someone else to take her place and the game starts again.

Ziziros (meaning 'cicada')

This is another chasing game. One child, Nicky, stands with his back to a group of children with his hands on one side of his face covering an ear. He stands there until one of the group touches his back while they all say 'Zz zz zz zz . . .' and spread about. Nicky, meanwhile, has turned round and chases about trying to catch someone by a touch of his finger. Whoever is caught takes Nicky's place

and they all position themselves to start again. This game is usually played on Easter Sunday. The noise made by the children is in imitation of the cicada.

Arnaki and Likos ('the lamb and the wolf')

Two children are chosen as the lamb and the wolf. The others stand in a circle with the wolf in the middle and the lamb outside. The wolf tries to escape from under the children's hands but they try to close the gap so that he doesn't escape. If he manages to get out the lamb comes into the circle and is protected by the circle. This continues until the wolf gets the lamb.

Traditionally this game is accompanied by chants. While the children are holding hands in a circle they all chant together,
   'Wolf, wolf are you there?'
The wolf replies,
   'I am here and I am going to catch you
   And when I do I will eat you up.'
He tries to get out of the circle.
The lamb says,
   'Wolf, wolf try to catch me if you can.'
The wolf replies,
   'I will, I will and when I do
   I will eat you up.'
The lamb and wolf taunt one another until the wolf succeeds in getting the lamb.

The lamb and the wolf   Arnaki ke likos

Greek folk song collected from Maria Roussou,
translated by Nitsa Sergides.
English lyrics by Jean Gilbert

Not too fast

1 Once there was a lit-tle lamb
   Mia fo-ra kie-na ke-ro
   Graz-ing near a lit-tle stream.
   se li-va-di dro-se ro

   He was hap-py graz-ing there
   En ar-na-ki to kai-me-no
   By the cool re-fresh-ing stream.
   e-vo-skou-se 'xe-nia-sme-no.

   But some bad luck came his way when
   O-mos ti-hi tou ka-ki
   He was spot-ted by a wolf.
   e-nas li-kos fta-nei-kei.

2 'I have caught you, I have seen
   You've been drinking from my stream.
   You must die for stealing my water
   You're the thief who comes to my stream.'
   'No, I was not drinking water,
   I was grazing by the stream.'

3 'You were rude about my shadow
   Cursing it one day last year.'
   'No, oh no, that was not me
   I was not even born last year.'
   'Well said, then it was your brother,
   I mistook you.' said the wolf.

4 'Please believe me, I'm the only one,
   I don't have a brother at home.'
   'That's a lie, you can't fool me,
   You will need a lawyer to win.'
   Then he opened wide his mouth
   And soon the little lamb was gone.

   (S'epiasa tou ipe eftis
   Klefti tha timorithis
   Irtes is ton potamo mou
   Ke mou pinis to neró mou)
   Ohi, ipe to arnaki
   Evlepa to livadaki.)

   (Omos persi ena vradi
   M'evrises mes to skotadi
   - Persi, ipe to kaimeno
   Ma den imoun gennimeno
   - Kala legis ego sfallo
   T'adelpaki sou to allo.)

   (Adelpákin sou omóno
   Pos den eho ime mono
   Tis psefties na tis afiseis
   Treha na dikigorisis
   Ke to stoma tou anigi
   Ke to distiho to pnigei.)

This song can be related to the game 'The lamb and
the wolf'. The children can be divided into two
groups to sing the two parts. Nitsa Sergides

remembers singing this little song to a tune very
similar to the one we know as 'Twinkle, twinkle
little star'. The English words sing well to this tune.

Won't you pass, Mistress Mary? Den pernas kira Maria

Greek folk song, translated by Susan and Ted Alevizos

2 I will go to the gardens,
   I won't pass, I won't pass,
   I will go to the gardens,
   I won't pass, pass, pass.

3 What will you do in the gardens,
   Won't you pass, won't you pass,
   What will you do in the gardens,
   Won't you pass, pass, pass?

4 I will cut two violets,
   I won't pass, I won't pass,
   I will cut two violets,
   I won't pass, pass, pass.

5 What will you do with the violets,
   Won't you pass, won't you pass,
   What will you do with the violets,
   Won't you pass, pass, pass?

6 I will give them to my favourite,
   I won't pass, I won't pass,
   I will give them to my favourite,
   I won't pass, pass, pass.

7 And who is your favourite,
   Won't you pass, won't you pass,
   And who is your favourite,
   Won't you pass, pass, pass?

8 My favourite is Georgia,
   I won't pass, I won't pass,
   My favourite is Georgia,
   I won't pass, pass, pass.

Suggested percussion

Verses 2, 4, 6, 8 –
solo or group singing

Verses 3, 5, 7 –
tambourine

Singing game

The children form a circle with 'Mistress Mary' on the outside. They walk round as they sing the questions and stop to listen to the answers sung by 'Mistress Mary' who could also have a little group to help her. At the last verse Mary stops in front of Georgia who then takes her place and the game begins again.

Alternatively, the children form a line with Mary in front, facing everyone. They walk to her and back again as they sing the questions and stand to listen to her answers. At the end Georgia joins Mary as the game continues. Eventually all the children in the first line have joined Mary's line.

Frail basil plant Psin trirasili

Cypriot folk song translated by Miltiades Erotokritou.
English lyrics by Jean Gilbert

Gently

1. Frail ba-sil plant, frail ba-sil plant, __ my gen-tle herb __ of __
Psin tri ra si li chi-a mou __ che man-tsou ra na

grace, Frail grace, You'll part me from my mo-ther, my
mou, Psin mou, E si tha me ho ri - sis a

gen-tle __ herb __ of __ grace, You'll grace.
pro tin - ma - na __ mou, E mou.

2 Oh come close by the window, my love come close to the glass, (repeat)
   So I can see your beauty shining from your face so fair. (repeat)

In this song the basil plant is compared to the
beauty of a young girl. Older children will
appreciate the fine melody of this beautiful folk
tune. It should be sung smoothly, clearly, not fast
and with attention to the phrasing.

Suggested accompaniment

chime bars, glockenspiel or metallophone

These chords support the guitar accompaniment.
Each chord could be played by:
one child holding three beaters *or* three children holding one beater each *or* two children sharing three beaters

Down to the beach   Rato sto yialo

Cypriot folk song, translated by Miltiades Erotokritou.
English lyrics by Jean Gilbert

2   There they go again
   To wash their clothes in the water, (repeat)
   Down to the beach to wash their clothes,
   Down to the beach to rub and scrub. (repeat)

3   And among those girls
   I see a dark-eyed beauty, (repeat)
   Down to the beach to wash their clothes,
   Down to the beach to rub and scrub. (repeat)

Suggested percussion

first four bars and repeat

tambourine

second four bars and repeat

Dance

The children dance in a ring holding hands.
Line 1 (and repeat)
16 walking or skipping steps to the right
Line 2
(first time)   four steps into the centre, kneel, four claps
(second time)   four steps back into the circle, four claps

Now repeat the dance walking or skipping to the left.

This is a very popular song in Cyprus and, as the lively tune suggests, is really a fun song about washing clothes on the beach. It invites further verses and could be adapted to describe the kind of things the children would do on the beach.

Jesus has risen   H'ristos anesti

Greek Easter hymn, translated by Nitsa Sergides

Oh Je - sus has ri - sen from the dead, And
H'ri - stos a - ne - sti eg - ne - gron Tha -

He has o - ver - come death, He has o - ver -
na - do tha - na - don ba di -

-come death, And of - fered e - ver -
- sas ge dis - en - dis mni ma -

-last - ing life e - ver - last - ing life.
- si zo - in ha - ri sa - me nos.

This Easter hymn is sung in all churches in Cyprus
on Easter Sunday. Sing it unaccompanied, very
clearly and not fast.

A fishing boat   Ksekina mia psaropoula

Greek folk song
translated by Miltiades Erotokritou.
English lyrics by Jean Gilbert

With spirit

2 On the boat are many brave men
   From the shore, from the shore;
   On the boat are many brave men,
   Men who dive deep down for sponges,
   Dive for black and beautiful coral,
   Deep down, deep down
   In the sea, in the sea.

   (Repeat)

3 May your journey prosper and bring you luck
   Brave fishing men, brave fishing men;
   May your journey prosper and bring you luck,
   May you bring back sponges from the deep,
   Bring us black and beautiful coral
   Back from the sea,
   Back from the deep, deep, blue sea.

   (Repeat)

Dance

This dance is called the 'Sirtos' and can be danced to the tune of this song. The traditional step fits a basic rhythm, common to this song, in this way:

left,   right, left,   right,   left, right

The left step is taken slightly to the left followed by two quicker steps (*right, left*) which move gently on the spot; then the right step is taken slightly to the right followed by the two quicker steps (*left, right*) moving also on the spot. The step could, if necessary, be simplified to:

left, and step right,   right, and step left

but the speed of the tune would need to be slightly quicker.

The dance pattern is as follows:

1 *Bars 1–6*   Partners in a circle dance six basic steps round in a circle holding partners' hands, and finish in two lines facing one another.

  Bars 7–10   Drop hands and take four small basic steps back in lines.

  Bars 11–14   Lines approach and cross over with four basic steps. They cover more ground and are now back facing.

  Bars 15–16   Lines take two basic steps back to rejoin partners.

2 *Bars 1–6*   As for 1.

  Bars 7–10   As for 1.

  Bars 11–12   Hands on hips. Children approach one another with two basic steps and stop alongside their partners in the line.

  Bars 13–14   Lines separate with two basic steps going back.

  Bars 15–16   Lines approach with two basic steps to rejoin partner.

3 *Bars 1–10*   As for 1.

  Bars 11–16   Leading couple in the line take opposite hands, facing, and dance round with six basic steps. Everyone else claps.

The dance could continue with other couples having a turn in the line as in the third variation. The traditional Sirtos continues with many other different variations.

Suggested dance accompaniment

tambourine

The 'Sirtos' dance can also be danced to the song 'Frail basil plant'.

Background information

The climax of the Christian festival of Easter comes in the holidays following the end of the Spring term; the dates vary as they depend upon the moon and the spring or vernal equinox. Easter Sunday is the Sunday following the first full moon on or after March 21st.

Although many schools remember the Easter story in their assemblies, most of the activities with younger children at this time of year are to do with the onset of Spring and remind us that the roots of this important festival are closely intertwined with the customs of our pagan ancestors. The word Easter comes from *Eostre*, the name of the goddess of Spring who was fêted, before Christianity came to northern Europe, every year at the time of the vernal equinox. Springtime, the time of new life and of warmer and longer days, is welcomed everywhere and must have been especially welcome to our ancestors. To Christians the resurrection of Jesus is a most joyous event; to many it symbolizes rebirth that in nature lies at the very roots of survival.

A number of our present day Easter customs have their origins in pagan fertility and nature rites and were adapted by the early Christians as part of their celebrations of the Feast of Easter; others are linked directly with events relating to the death and resurrection of Jesus.

The egg has always been a symbol of fertility and new life and plays an important part in Christian Easter celebrations. It was customary to give hen or goose eggs with their shells painted or dyed in bright colours. The Saturday before Ash Wednesday was once called Egg Saturday; this was when children went begging for eggs that had to be eaten up before Lent. They also begged for eggs after Lent when they looked forward to eating them again. The eggs were called 'pace' eggs from the French word 'Pâques' meaning Easter. In many villages (hard-boiled) egg-rolling contests were held on Easter Monday. Today children bring decorated hard-boiled eggs to school for egg and spoon races. The chocolate egg only dates back about one hundred years.

The eating of hot cross buns can be traced to pre-Christian spring celebrations in Roman times when small wheaten cakes were prepared, divided into four sections by a cross representing the four quarters of the phases of the moon. The cross on the Easter bun now symbolizes the Cross on Calvary. It was a custom to eat these buns hot from the bakers, though 'hot' may also refer to their spicy flavour.

Wearing new clothes is a traditional feature of many festivals; at Easter they are worn in honour of Christ. Traditionally a complete set of new clothes was worn at church for old clothes were said to bring bad luck. Poor people overcame this belief by wearing at least one new item, usually a hat for women and a scarf or gloves for men. Today an Easter Bonnet Parade is held in many parts of the country when ladies and girls parade through local parks or streets wearing elaborate head gear they have designed and made themselves. Many schools do the same *and* include the boys!

Art and craft

Things to do with hard-boiled eggs

1 Cover with felt-tip patterns. Varnish or spray with a fixative to preserve.
2 Turn into people or animals, improvising additions like hats, hair, ears, feet, etc.
3 Cover with Copydex and press on small squares of cotton cloth to get a patchwork effect, or any kind of small trinkets like beads, buttons, or even small seeds. Aim for an overall design.
4 Shell the eggs and use the broken shells for mosaics.

To get a coloured base for any of the above ideas first drop the eggs into a cold water dye.

Cress people

Carefully crack a fresh egg and use the empty half shells to grow cress. Improvise faces.

Easter bonnets

There are a number of different ways of making decorated or funny hats. The basis can be strong card or discarded winter woolly 'pull-ons' or berets. Here are some suggestions:

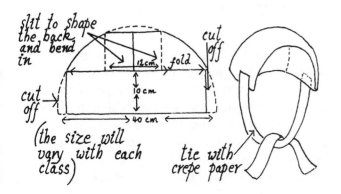

The basis of the bonnet is a semi-circular piece of card. The back folds can be bent in and stuck and crepe paper attached for tying. The bonnet is then ready for decorating.

A simplified version can be made from a long strip of card – the main strip shown in the diagram above. Streamers can be hung from the back to mask the head and the strip then decorated. Attach crepe ribbons for tying.

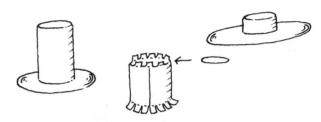

The hat can be made from two shapes – the tube measured to fit the head and the brim, cut from a large or small piece of circular card and stuck to the head piece which is splayed at the bottom. A top can be fitted, but is not really necessary especially as it will probably be covered by decorations. Use crepe ribbons for tying if necessary.

The beret or woolly hat can become the basis for an Easter creation. Card to hold further decoration can be stuck or stapled on, or the hat itself can be covered.

Miscellaneous

1 Make Easter cards including some large class ones to send to people like the caretaker, the lollipop man/lady, or to places like the local hospital children's ward and the local children's library.
2 Make an Easter basket from a plastic carton covered with crumpled tissue; decorate a small strip of card for the handle.
3 Draw plants and flowers from life. This will sharpen the children's observation and stimulate discussion about growth.

139

4 Grow as many different kinds of seeds as possible.
5 Start gardening in earnest if your school can allot you any patches of ground to cultivate.
6 Make a study of a small creature like a baby chick, a tadpole, a kitten or a lamb if you are near a farm.
7 Cook some Easter goodies.

Festival food

Simnel cake

These cakes were taken as gifts when sons and daughters who had left home were given a holiday on the fourth Sunday in Lent to visit their mothers. In the Christian calendar this Sunday is known as Mothering Sunday, though it was in earlier times a day especially dedicated to Mother Church and reflects a very old pre-Christian festival that celebrated the 'Mother of the Gods'. Our present Mother's Day is, in fact, an adopted American tradition. Bunches of flowers are given and in some families mothers are given a day off when someone else cooks the dinner.

150g (6 oz) plain flour
1 teaspoon baking powder
100g (4 oz) sugar
100g (4 oz) butter or margarine
3 eggs
100g (4 oz) sultanas
100g (4 oz) currants and raisins
50g (2 oz) chopped mixed peel
½ teaspoon mixed spice
pinch salt
200g (8 oz) almond paste
royal icing sufficient for a small round in the centre

METHOD
1 Cream sugar and butter and add beaten eggs (save a little for brushing the cake top later).
2 Add sifted flour, salt, baking powder if necessary.
3 Stir in dried fruit, peel and spice.
4 Put half the cake mixture into a lined cake tin. Spread over about a third of the almond paste and cover with the rest of the cake mixture.
5 Bake in a moderately slow oven (325°F Regulo mark 3) for about 2½ hours or until done. Leave to cool.

6 Cover the top with the rest of the almond paste saving a little to make some small eggs to go round the top. Brush with watered beaten egg and return to a hot oven for a few minutes.
7 Make a small round platform of icing in the centre. Let the children decide how to decorate (small 'sweet' eggs, smarties baby chicks, etc.).

A simnel cake could be improvised from a bought fruit cake, almond paste and suitable decoration.

Easter biscuits

75g (3 tablespoons) butter or margarine
65g (2 tablespoons) caster sugar
1 large egg
175g (1½ cups) self-raising flour
pinch of salt
40g (1–2 tablespoons) currants
15g (½ tablespoon) mixed peel
30ml (2 tablespoons) milk
15g (½ tablespoon) granulated sugar

METHOD
1 Cream the butter and caster sugar.
2 Separate the egg and beat in the yolk.
3 Sift the flour with the salt and fold into creamed mixture with the currants and mixed peel.
4 Add enough milk to make a fairly soft dough, cover and leave in a cool place to firm.
5 Knead lightly on a floured board and roll out to about ½ cm thickness.
6 Use shaped cutters to make individual biscuits – about 20.
7 Put on greased baking trays and bake for about 20 minutes in a warm oven at 350°F (180°C), gas mark 4.
8 After ten minutes, brush biscuits with the egg white, sprinkle with the granulated sugar and continue cooking until lightly coloured.

Movement

This reflects the dominant theme of this section, that of new life. Children in both town and country will be able to watch spring flowers appear and trees gradually come into leaf. Country children are more fortunate when it comes to closer contact with nature. However, most schools are able to keep tadpoles and some town children can even watch baby chicks hatch and grow when interested

teachers make arrangements for their school to
adopt some fertilized eggs and rear the chicks. The
following suggestions extend this interest into
movement:

Theme	Movement	Suggested accompaniment	
Growing plants			
The seed	tightly curled up bodies begin to move very slowly all over	silence sand block or drum head scratched	
The shoot appears	kneeling bodies, hands bringing the arms upwards one hand, the shoot, peeps above the head	continue until the 'shoot' appears finger cymbal or triangle	
The shoot grows	children slowly stand up bringing their arms above their heads	gentle tambourine rustle	
The flower opens	children slowly take up the shape of a flower or plant	slow notes quietly played on chime bars or glockenspiel	
Hatching eggs			
The chicks are inside their shells	any curled up position	quiet cymbal 'shiver'	
They break their shells	tiny movements at first then short, sharp movements all over until the 'beak' breaks through	clappers, castanets or wood block triangle	
The chicks are born	bodies uncurl, arms as wings unfold, every part shakes in turn	shakers, sand block	
They explore their world and find Mother Hen	children stagger to their feet, try to preen, wobble around and finally settle under the hen	tambourine cymbal 'shiver'	

The children could move in groups of about six around one child who could improvise as
Mother Hen.

Tadpoles and frogs			
The spawn floats in the water like lumpy jelly covered with black spots	curled up bodies in small groups moving very slightly	quiet cymbal 'shiver' the occasional sound from a chime bar or glockenspiel	
The spots get bigger and the jelly spreads	children move gently away from one another as they uncurl	continue with a little more animation	

The tadpoles come to life	children in turn dart away from the group as their strong tails wiggle	ripples on the xylophone followed by random struck notes and then a cymbal clash	
	they wiggle, dart around and then 'freeze', continuing like this until they are all moving		
They turn into frogs	the wiggling and darting movements gradually become hops on two feet with bended knees and legs wide apart	jump from note to note on the xylophone	
	the jumps get bigger and stronger	drum or tambour	

Some teachers may prefer to use just one instrument when accompanying movement; it is certainly easier. The most versatile instrument for this is a good tambourine which can be struck, rustled, scratched, tapped and tinkled! Otherwise assemble the instruments you are going to use and choose one or two reliable children to help. This is good training for them and the use of a variety of sounds can link up with any sound picture work you may do.

Recorded music can be incorporated as listening or as an accompaniment, though for the latter purpose it is not always as precise as directed percussion. The electronic rendering of Debussy's *Snowflakes are falling* by Tomita gives a 'watery' sound. 'Hens and cocks' from *Carnival of the Animals* by Saint-Saëns, 'The Hen' by Respighi and 'Hatching Chicks' from *Pictures at an Exhibition* by Mussorgsky can all be used for hen and chick movements.

Sound pictures

These could be based on the ideas for 'suggested accompaniment' in the preceding movement section.

Music corner

Mount pictures of the children's drawings and paintings that illustrate the themes you have covered in your movement sessions and the sound pictures you have made.

Sound pictures

Leave out the instruments you have used so that the children can continue with their own improvisations following the ideas already introduced. They could work in small groups of two, three or four for this.

Making up tunes

Choose a simple couplet from one of the poems or one written by a child. Introduce this activity with your class or group first:
1 Say the words rhythmically several times.
2 Clap and say the words.
3 Clap and whisper the words.
4 Play a tune on the chime bars using that rhythm.
5 Ask the children to sing the tune.
6 Let a few children have a turn; always sing the tune.

Prepare a simple work card and leave with the chime bars in the music corner.

e.g.

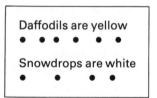

Tune using notes D E G A:

Playing by ear

Suggestions are given in the songs 'New life in spring' and 'Down in the forest'.

It is the joyful Easter time

Traditional carol (*I saw three ships*), words by A.M. Milner-Barry

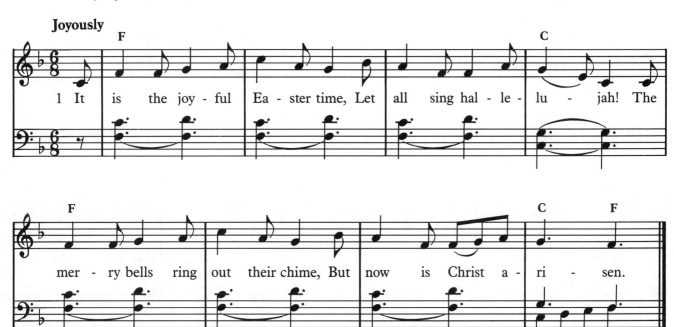

Joyously

1 It is the joy-ful Ea-ster time, Let all sing hal-le-lu – jah! The

mer-ry bells ring out their chime, But now is Christ a-ri – sen.

2 The world is bright with flowers gay,
   And all Christ's people praise and pray,
   For Jesus rose on Easter Day,
      Sing joyful hallelujah!

Suggested accompaniments

The following bars can introduce the song and also
be played in between the verses:

chime bars or glockenspiel

The following accompaniment played on chime
bars or glockenspiel can accompany the verses:

When Easter to the dark world came

Traditional melody arranged by June Boyce.
Words by W.H. Hamilton

2 When Mary in the garden walked,
   And with her risen Master talked:
   At Eastertide. . .

3 And friend to friend in wonder said:
   'The Lord is risen from the dead!'
   At Eastertide . . .

4 This Eastertide with joyful voice
   We'll sing 'The Lord is King! rejoice!'
   At Eastertide . . .

Guitar Older children may prefer to sing in a higher key. Guitar chords for the key of G are indicated in brackets.

Round for the coming of Spring

Traditional, arranged by June Boyce

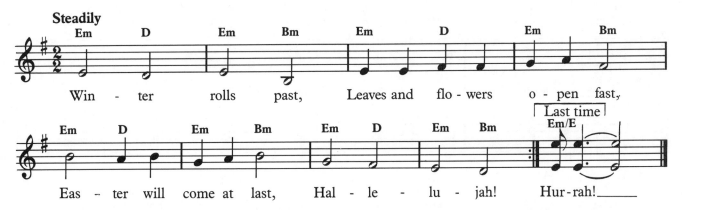

Take this round at a steady pace; make sure that the tune is really well known before you attempt to sing it as a round. Be satisfied with a two-part round unless your group is really confident, and enlist the help of another adult or older child to ensure a successful first attempt.

Rounds should be sung unaccompanied, but you may prefer to teach this initially with the guitar or a simple melodic accompaniment on the piano or tuned percussion. The suggested ostinato will underline the pulse and could also be used to maintain the rhythm once the round singing is established.

It is a good idea to vary the singing with each repeat to add musical interest. One way of singing this one would be:

1st time – very quietly
2nd time – clearly and positively
3rd time – firmly, slightly louder

This way there will be a gradual crescendo (getting louder) but the speed should be constant.

The round can end with each part finishing one by one and with everyone joining in the 'Hurrah!'. Alternatively you could stop with an agreed signal when everyone is singing, then add the 'Hurrah!' after a short pause.

Suggested accompaniment

chime bars or xylophone

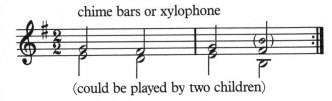

(could be played by two children)

New life in Spring

Music by Christopher Bruce, words by Geoffrey Duncan.
Slightly adapted by Jean Gilbert

Quietly at first

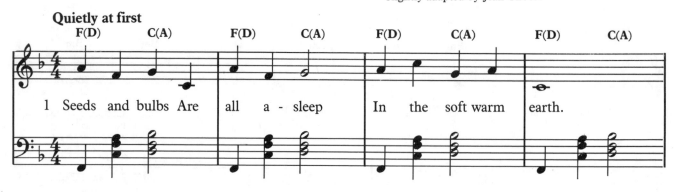

1 Seeds and bulbs Are all a - sleep In the soft warm earth.

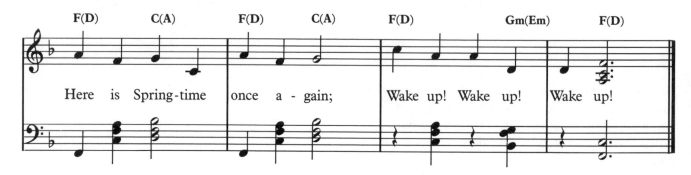

Here is Spring-time once a - gain; Wake up! Wake up! Wake up!

2 Sun and rain
  Begin their work
  On the soft warm earth.
  Here is Springtime once again;
  Wake up! Wake up! Wake up!

3 Springtime flowers
  Begin to wake
  From the soft warm earth.
  Here is Springtime once again;
  New life! New life! New life!

4 Everywhere
  New life begins,
  Flowers and lambs and birds.
  Here is Springtime once again;
  New life! New life! New life!

Verse for Easter Day:

5 Jesus lives
  For everyone
  Over all the earth.
  Here is Easter once again;
  New life! New life! New life!

Suggested percussion

 finger cymbal or triangle (last line)

 quiet tambourine (last line)

 tambourine (last line)

 tambourine (last line)

146

Suggested accompaniment

OR

These accompaniments can be played on any tuned
percussion instrument, but if you can use more than
one instrument the following arrangement could
support the gradual build-up as the verses proceed:

Verse 1   accompaniment 1 on soprano glockenspiel
Verse 2   accompaniment 2 on soprano glockenspiel
Verse 3   accompaniment 2 on chime bars
Verse 4   accompaniment 1 on chime bars
              accompaniment 2 on xylophone
Verse 5   continue

Playing by ear

When the children know the song well, show them
how to play the first two lines:

> Seeds and bulbs are all asleep
> A   F G   C A F G

Point out that this phrase is made of two groups of
notes A   F   G joined by low C.

Guitar is easier in D (chords in brackets) capoed up
three frets. Alternatively play in D and sing at a
lower pitch, which might suit younger children.

The little seed

Christina Brice

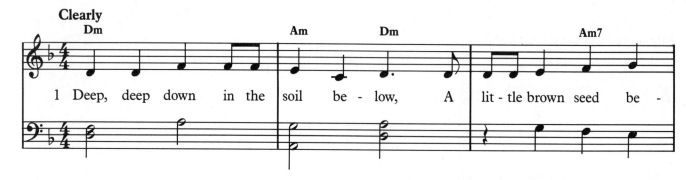

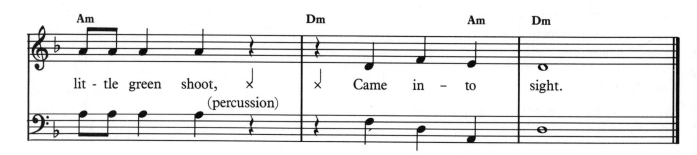

Suggested percussion

2 Taller, taller the green shoot grew,
  The sun shone down and the warm wind blew,
  Down came cooling showers of rain.
  And the warm sun shone
  On the earth again.

 chime bar A

3 Tall green shoot standing firm on the ground,
  Saw many shoots like himself around,
  Waving 'neath the bright blue sky
  While a passing breeze
  Made a rustling sigh.

 shakers

4 Golden all the shoots became,
  With nodding heads all looked the same;
  A field of yellow, waving corn,
  Like a golden sea
  In the summer's morn.

bells

Recorders

The tune lies within the range of the descant recorder and is easy enough for an older child to play. The following accompaniment can be played on the chimes or descant recorder.

Movement

The life of the growing seed is clearly outlined in the words of this song which could become the basis for movement to do with growth in the spring.

Verse 1
Very tightly curled up bodies – slowly uncurl, imagining the feet as roots and the arms as shoots. The children try to feel the impact of the first shoot pushing through the upper soil.

Verse 2
The arms gradually push higher, though still tightly entwined.

Verses 3 and *4*
The arms unfold and stretch up stiffly, then gradually loosen and sway to and fro. The children look round and nod their heads as the breeze blows.

The sun
Slowly open arms out as if drawing a big circle; then move around slowly and smoothly occasionally turning round on the spot.

The rain
The cooling showers can be represented by the arms gently coming down, the hands 'shivering'. The children can tiptoe round making high to low movements.

The breeze
Swaying movements extended through the arms. The children can move about slowly stopping to sway from time to time.

The song could be sung by one group of children while another group performs the seed 'ballet'. Divide the dancers into seeds, sun(s), breezes and showers. The seeds could 'grow' in the middle responding to the elements that could move in an outer circle. (See also the poem 'Seed song'.)

Sound picture

Tell the story in sound.

Storyline		Suggested sound makers
The seed grows underground		sand block or gently scrape a drum head
The little green shoot pushes through the soil		triangle or finger cymbal
The shoot grows		shakers
The sun		cymbal played with a padded beater – sustained by chime bars
Wind		voices
Breeze		quiet shakers
Showers		bells
The nodding heads of corn		quiet wood blocks or clappers

You could end the sound picture with the waving corn 'sounding' beneath a sunny sky with a light breeze coming and going.

The musicians could also adapt their music to accompany the seed 'ballet', giving yet another interpretation.

Spring is coming

Christina Brice, words adapted by Jean Gilbert

2   Spring is coming everywhere,
    Birds sing in the branches bare,
    Snowdrop shyly hangs her head,
    Spring is here and winter's dead.
        Spring is here, spring is here,
        See all the new life everywhere. (repeat)

3   Spring is coming everywhere,
    Bright the day and fresh the air;
    Town and country greet the sun,
    Children play when work is done.
        Spring is here, spring is here,
        See all the new life everywhere. (repeat)

Perhaps your children can think of another verse to describe what they like to do in Spring.

Percussion

Add a crisp tambourine beat in the last two lines of each verse:

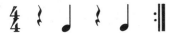

Spring dance

Arrange the children in groups of two circles, a smaller circle inside a bigger one; for practising just have two large circles. The basic step is a jaunty walk; the tempo must be fairly brisk for this.

Large circle
Verses 1, 2, and 3
lines 1 and 2 – eight jaunty steps to the left
lines 3 and 4 – eight jaunty steps to the right
line 5 – clap facing a partner
line 6 – circle with a partner

Smaller circle
Verse 1
lines 1 and 2 – children crouch down and pretend to 'grow'
lines 2 and 3 – circle on the spot with arms lifted upward
lines 5 and 6 – as for the large circle

Verse 2
lines 1 and 2 – some children stand as trees or birds
lines 3 and 4 – the rest become snowdrops
lines 5 and 6 – as for the large circle

Verse 3
as for the large circle but travel in the opposite direction

Add a tambourine beat to emphasize the rhythm for the dancers.

Guitar   Guitarists might prefer to play in D. Capo up three frets to sing in the key of F.

Easter Trip

Words and music by Jane Morgan

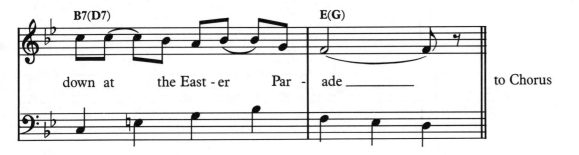

down at   the East - er   Par - ade _____   to Chorus

2   I have made an Easter top hat,
    See the decorations on it,
    I'll be happy when I'm dressed up in it
    Down at the Easter parade.

This song invites more verses about what the
children have made and can wear 'down at the
Easter Parade'.

Suggested percussion

Chorus

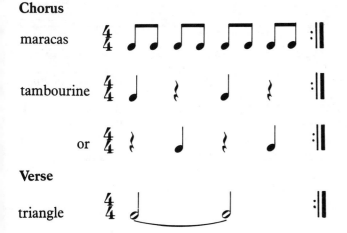

maracas

tambourine

or

Verse

triangle

Guitar   The chords in brackets enable teachers to
play in a higher key without using a capo.

Pace egg song

Traditional West Yorkshire song, collected in Midgley by Roy Palmer

Steadily

VERSES I AND 5

1 Come search up your mo - ney, Be ju - bi - lant and free, And__

give us your pace egg For Eas - ter Mon - day. *Fine*

VERSES 2, 3, 4

2 Go__ down to your cel - lars And see what you'll find, If your

bar - rels be emp - ty I hope you'll pro - vide; I

hope you'll pro - vide___ Sweet eggs and strong beer, And we'll

come no more to you Un - til the next year. time.

1-2   3 *D.C. al Fine*

3 These times they are hard
   And money is scant,
   But one pace egg of yours
   Is all that we want;
   And if you will grant us
   This little small thing,
   We'll all charm our voices
   And merry we'll sing.

4 Just look at St George
   So brisk and so bold,
   While in his right hand
   A sword he doth hold;
   A star on his breast
   Like silver doth shine,
   And I hope you'll remember
   It's pace egging time.

5 Come search up your money
   And see that it's right:
   If you give now't we'll take now't
   Farewell and goodnight.

This song is sung by boys from the Calder High
School, Mytholmroyd, at the end of their Pace Egg
play which is performed in the streets of the local
towns and villages every Good Friday.

More songs for Easter time

Sing-a-Song One (Nelson)

This collection has a section of suitable spring songs and stories mainly for younger children. It includes:

> The little seed
> Spring song
> Cowboy Spring
> The tree in the wood
> The enormous turnip

Singing Fun
by Lucille F. Wood and Louise B. Scott (Harrap)

Another Spring section for younger children:

> Easter bunny
> A green frog
> My Easter bonnet
> Pussy willow
> Little seeds
> Springtime

Wonderful World
by Christina R. Brice from *Ways with Music* (Chappell)

These songs are for older children. Two springlike ones are:

> Dance yellow daffodil (lovely for movement)
> Welcome Spring

Someone's singing, Lord (A. & C. Black)

Songs for Palm Sunday:

> Hurray for Jesus
> We have a king who rides a donkey (to the tune of 'What shall we do with the drunken sailor?')
> Morning has broken (Eleanor Farjeon wrote the words of this popular assembly song for the first day of Spring. Its theme is recreation.)

Their words my thoughts (O.U.P.)

This collection containing hymns, songs, thoughts and poems is for older children. Among the hymns outlining the Easter story are several suitable for lower and middle juniors:

> Ride on! Ride on in majesty!
> Trotting, trotting through Jerusalem
> There is a green hill

Harlequin (A. & C. Black)

Here is a mixed selection:

> Shrove Tuesday
> Snowdrop bells
> Pussy willow
> Spring has sprung
> It happens each spring
> My Easter bonnet (with extra verses)
> April

Poems

Eastertide

Here's two or three jolly boys
    All of one mind,
We've come a pace-egging,
    And hope you'll be kind;
We hope you'll be kind
    With your eggs and your beer,
And we'll come no more pace-egging
    Until the next year.

Traditional rhyme

The blossom

The blossom fell – weary of holding the twig,
Slowly – it parachuted to the ground
Like an aeroplane
Circling an airport.
The blossom circled the gutter
Landing on a cushion of grass cuttings,
An apple core for a pillow,
A crisp bag for a pillow.
The delicate blossom stood out amongst the rubbish,
A car rambled past – its exhaust pipe blowing madly
Eager to be on its way
The blossom followed the car
Carried by the passing wind
But the car soon overtook
And was gone forever.
Another car came by
Before the wind could catch it
The blossom was squashed on the front wheel
Stuck by its own juices
When next the wheel turned
A lone petal floated down
Stained with dirt.

Jenny Saffran

Welcome to Spring

I have heard a mother bird
Singing in the rain –
Telling all her little ones
Spring has come again!

I have seen a wave of green
Down a lovely lane –
Making all the hedges glad
Spring has come again!

I have found a patch of ground
Golden in the sun;
Crocuses are calling out
Spring has just begun!

Irene Thompson

Snowdrops

I like to think
    That, long ago
There fell to earth
    Some flakes of snow
Which loved this cold
    Grey world of ours
So much, they stayed
    As snowdrop flowers.

Mary Vivian

Seed song

This is a story about a seed
Lying in the ground
Which slept right through the
wintertime
Till Springtime came around.

When all at once the sunshine came
And drops of gentle rain,
The ground became much warmer
And the seed woke up again.

Then from the seed there grew a root
Which wriggled in the ground;
Root from the seed,
That wonderful seed
Way down in the ground.

Then from the root there came a shoot
Which came up for some air;
Shoot from the root
Root from the seed
That wonderful seed
Way down in the ground.

Then from the shoot there came a leaf
When the sun began to shine;
Leaf from the shoot,
Shoot from the root,
Root from the seed,
That wonderful seed
Way down in the ground.

Then from the leaf there came a plant
Watered by the roots;
Plant from the leaf,
Leaf from the shoot,
Shoot from the root,
Root from the seed,
That wonderful seed
Way down in the ground.

Then from the plant there came a bud
As summer came around;
Bud from the plant,
Plant from the leaf,
Leaf from the shoot,
Shoot from the root,
Root from the seed,
That wonderful seed
Way down in the ground.

Then from the bud there came a
flower
To greet the summer sun;
Flower from the bud,
Bud from the plant,
Plant from the leaf,
Leaf from the shoot,
Shoot from the root,
Root from the seed,
That wonderful seed
Way down in the ground.

But when at last the Autumn came
And leaves fell all around,
A new seed ripened in the flower
And then dropped to the ground.
The seed slipped back into the earth
Washed by the gentle rain
And slept right through the
wintertime
Till Spring came around again.

Christopher Rowe

Easter present

'Tomorrow it's Easter and I've got an egg
That's bigger than anyone else's', said Leigh.
'It's a large chocolate football and filled up with sweets
And you are all going to be jealous of me.'

But we were not jealous, for our Easter eggs
Were set under our hen and she kept them so warm
That when the sun rose, seven small yellow chicks
Had pecked their way out of the shells and were born.

And now one week later, Leigh's present has gone.
He ate it so fast and was sick after tea.
But our little chicks are still lovely and bright
And they're living and *real* and that's Easter for me.

Jess Curtis

A play with music

The story of Persephone

Characters
Persephone, the Spirit of the Spring
Demeter, Mother Earth, mother of Persephone
Pluto, God of the Underworld called Hades
God of the Sea
God of the Sun
Goddess of the Moon
God of the Sky
Hermes, Messenger of the Gods
Persephone's friends – maidens and shepherds
Forest animals, trees and birds
Shades and shadows, Spirits of the Underworld
Narrator

Music – recorded or children's improvisations, see
page 159–160.

Enter **Narrator** to *recorded music* **a** or *cymbal and drum beat*.
The narrator introduces the play and explains that a long time ago nobody understood why the seasons changed, why Spring followed Winter. They made up stories about the things they didn't understand and the story of Persephone was a Greek story about the return of Spring every year. Exit.

Enter **Persephone** and her **friends** (*recorded music* **a** or *improvised percussion*).
The young people have come to meet, chat and play with the forest animals. *More music*.

Enter **Demeter** to the same music which stops as everyone sits down.
Demeter says that she has been busy gardening and seeing to all the new plants that have begun to grow. She has come for a

rest. Persephone asks her to see their spring dance. (Use *recorded music* **b** or the *dance arrangement* to the song 'Spring is coming'

with a singing group.) Demeter applauds. They all exit to the same music, humming, laughing or singing as they go.

Enter **Narrator** to set the next scene.
One day when Persephone was wandering by herself, she was seized by Pluto, God of the Underworld, to be his queen.

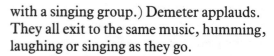

Enter **Persephone** to *recorded music* **a** or *quiet percussion – bells and triangles*.
She wanders round picking flowers. Suddenly there is a loud cymbal crash and banging of drums. Pluto comes in with his attendants and seizes Persephone. She is frightened and is pulled away struggling. *Recorded music* **c** or *drum and cymbal*.

SILENCE

Demeter is heard calling Persephone. She enters. First of all she is cross, but as she continues calling she realizes that Persephone is lost. Persephone's friends enter and Demeter asks them if they know where Persephone is, but no one has seen her. Demeter says that she will ask the

Gods. The friends exit and Demeter walks slowly to one side (*slow drum beat*).

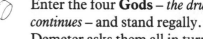
Enter the four **Gods** – *the drum beat continues* – and stand regally.
Demeter asks them all in turn if they know where her daughter is. The God of the Sun, the last one to be asked, says that he saw Pluto seize her and take her to Hades to be Queen of the Underworld. The Gods exit

leaving Demeter grief stricken (*drum beat* or *recorded music* **d**). Demeter walks slowly and sadly round and off as the music continues.

Enter **Narrator** to *recorded music* **d** or *drum beat* to say that as time went on and Persephone remained underground, the earth became sad and cold. Plants died, there was no harvest and people starved and died. The God of the Sky ordered Pluto to return Persephone to her mother if she had not eaten any of the fruit of the dead.

Enter **Pluto, Persephone** and the **Shades** to *recorded music* **e** or *slow drum beat*. They walk slowly: Persephone is sad. Pluto and Persephone sit down on their thrones. They are offered food to eat. Persephone refuses to eat. The Shades move slowly on one side and watch.

Enter **Demeter**. She says she has come at the command of the God of the Sky to take Persephone back. Pluto reminds her of the one condition – that Persephone should not have eaten any food of the Underworld. Demeter asks her daughter if she has eaten anything. Persephone remains sad and silent. Demeter asks again and goes to get Persephone. Then one of the Shades comes forward and says that he saw Queen Persephone eat some pomegranate seeds.

Persephone points to a bowl of fruit; Pluto picks up a pomegranate which has been bitten into and says that some seeds have been eaten. Persephone speaks at last. She just says that she has eaten five seeds.

Demeter walks away sadly. Everyone exits to a *slow drum beat* or *recorded music* **d**.

Enter some flower children, trees, birds and animals.

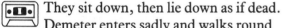

They sit down, then lie down as if dead. Demeter enters sadly and walks round looking at all the dead things (*recorded music* **d** or *drum beat*). A cymbal announces the God of the Sky who enters and tells Demeter that he has decided that

Persephone should return to earth as everything is dying without her, but that she should go back to the Underworld for part of the year – one month for every pomegranate seed she had eaten. He will send Hermes to bring her back. He goes and Demeter waits (some bright music – *recorded music* **b** or *bells and triangles* – is heard). Enter Hermes with Persephone. Mother and daughter embrace. As they walk happily round looking at the flowers, trees and forest creatures, these gradually sit up and come to life. Persephone's friends come to greet her and the scene finishes with the same spring dance that the play started with.

Suggestions for recorded music a and **introductory music**
'Morning' from *Peer Gynt Suite* No. 1 Op. 46 by Grieg

b
'Anitra's Dance' from *Peer Gynt Suite* No. 3 Op. 46

This music would require a freer dance arrangement than the spring dance already outlined. The music suggests a running step for young children. The girls could run freely in and out of the boys who could play tambourines to the beat – it is 3-time and would invite an 'um-pa-pa' sound. The girls could occasionally turn round on the spot or turn round with a partner.

c
'In the hall of the mountain king' from *Peer Gynt Suite* No. 4 Op. 46
Fade in to the last part of this number where the music is more turbulent than dance-like.

d
'Åse's death' from *Peer Gynt Suite* No. 2 Op. 46

e
'Solveig's song' from *Peer Gynt Suite* No. 4 Op. 55

Costumes for the play can be very simple:
Persephone – a summer dress, green if possible
Demeter – a summer dress, brown if possible and a cloak to wrap around when mourning for Persephone
The Gods – crowns and cloaks of a suitable colour
Hermes – crown and wings attached to sandals
Maidens and shepherds – summer dresses and shorts and shirts
Animals, trees, birds, flowers – head-dresses
Shades and shadows – grey and black tights and T-shirts

For a more elaborate production Greek costumes for people and gods and all-over costumes for animals, trees and flowers might be more appropriate. It will depend upon resources and the occasion.

Improvisations

Lively music (for the entrance of Persephone and her friends)
Use a skipping rhythm on the xylophone and support with notes on the beat from the chime bars or glockenspiel.

xylophone

chime bars or glockenspiel

tambourine or bells

play   and   skip   and dance

The repeat tune on the chime bars could begin and play all the way through. The xylophone could enter when ready and repeat as necessary. The words are only to help the xylophone player and, of course, it is best to allow the player to improvise to produce his own tune. It will all depend upon the experience and ability of the children.

Sad music (if required)
Use lower notes and play slowly in a descending or coming down sequence. Underline with a slow drum beat.

Background information

Eid-ul-Fitr is an important Muslim festival which marks the end of Ramadan, a month of fasting. It is a celebration of about three days as a token of thanksgiving to Allah. The precise dates differ each year as the Muslim calendar is based upon the lunar months and the Islamic year is shorter than the western one, but it always takes place on the first day of the tenth Muslim month. In 1989 the festival was in May.

Throughout the month of Ramadan all adult Muslims in good health abstain from food and drink during the hours of daylight. The rules are strictly obeyed especially by devout Muslims; much of the time is spent in prayer. Sick people and those travelling on long journeys are allowed to eat but they are expected to fast later, when they are able. The purpose of the fast is to teach the value of physical and mental self-discipline, to enable those who are rich to experience poverty and to set a standard of behaviour for the rest of the year.

Fasting is one of the compulsory duties for Muslims. These are known as the Five Pillars of Islam and are:

1 Belief in the oneness of Allah (God) and the prophet Muhammad (Peace Be Unto Him).
2 Making regular prayers, five times a day.
3 Fasting during the month of Ramadan.
4 Paying Zakat, a donation of income as alms.
5 Going on a pilgrimage to Mecca at least once in a life time.

The religion of Islam was founded by the prophet Muhammad who, it is believed, first heard the voice of Allah through the Angel Gabriel in 610 A.D. when he was meditating in the hills near Mecca, his native city. He continued to receive revelations in a number of visions over a period of about 23 years. The messages, memorized by Muhammad and later dictated to scribes, became the Qur'an or Koran, the holy book of Islam. The revelation of the Qur'an to Muhammad is commemorated on the 27th day of Ramadan when there is a special 'night of power' called Lailat-ul-Qadr.

On the morning of the festival of Eid-ul-Fitr everyone bathes and puts on new or thoroughly clean clothes. They then assemble at the local mosque or at a (clean) meeting place for the first prayers of the day. In some communities it will be the men who attend the mosque. This is followed by a celebration meal with the rest of the family; visits are made to friends and happy greetings are exchanged. It is an especially happy time for children as they look forward to receiving gifts from older members of the family. People send Eid cards and are expected to give money to the poor and needy.

Art and craft

The making of Eid cards can be based on pattern and design in Islamic art. Muslims do not accept any form of representational art so drawings of Muhammad or any of the other prophets are strictly forbidden. It would be a good idea to show the children an Eid greeting card. This could be bought from an Asian shop or possibly borrowed from a local resources unit. Perhaps, if you teach any Muslim children, one of them could bring a card from home.

Here are a few suggestions on which patterns for your Eid cards could be based.

Festival food

Each group of Muslims will have the food and cuisine of the country in which they live. In India festival foods will include Barphi and Samosas, as described in the section on Diwali.

The following recipe from Mrs Alam comes from Bengal and, apart from the frying, can be made by the children:

Dimer pita

100g (4 oz) rice flour
100g (4 oz) sugar
2 small eggs
Pinch salt

METHOD
1 Mix flour, sugar and salt together.
2 Beat the eggs and add very gradually to the flour mixture until it handles like dough. If too wet add a little more flour.
3 Roll out gently to about ½ cm thickness – no thinner.
4 Cut into shapes with biscuit cutters or a knife or make some little balls.
5 Fry in fairly deep vegetable oil in a chip pan until light golden on both sides. The little biscuits will puff up in the hot oil. Keep turning them and make sure they remain well covered in oil. This takes about four to five minutes. This amount will make about two dozen small biscuity cakes.

The foods mentioned in the song 'A beautiful day' are:

Korma

This is a rich substantial dish of braised chicken and vegetables with added cream or yoghurt and without chilli powder. The term 'korma' also refers to one of the most important techniques in Indian cooking, that of braising, using the minimum of cooking liquor which is absorbed back into the meat during very slow cooking. Aromatic flavours are added in three stages: during the marinade, half way through the cooking and towards the end.

Pulau

Indian pulau is related to paella and risotto. Plain pulau is a savoury rice made by frying washed rice in some ghee or clarified butter and then cooking it in a stock until the liquid is fully absorbed.

Firni

This is a rice compote, a sweet dessert. It consists of ground rice cooked with milk and sugar like a thick rice pudding. Rose water is added just before it is fully set. It is served chilled in small shallow dishes and scattered with slivered almonds and pistachio nuts.

Prayer to the Prophet Muhammad

Traditional first verse.
Additional verse translated from Bengali by
Hiron Alam (verse 2) and Nur Chowdhury (verses 3 and 4)

Unaccompanied

1 Ya na - bi sa - lam a - lay - ka____ Ya ra -

(Arabic)

- sul sa - lam a - lay - ka____ Ya ha -

- bib sa - lam a - lay - ka____ Sa - la

wa - tul - la a - lay - ka.____

2   For the sun and moon shine in the sky,
       But that light does not shine bright enough
       And my heart is filled with light from you
       Like a new sun in the sky of my mind.

3   With your light divine the world is awake,
       And the nightingale is singing again;
       See the flowers have started blossoming
       And the world is filled with light and joy.

4   I am not a prophet – only a child,
       Not an angel nor a prophet of God,
       So I give my thanks to God because
       He has made me one of your followers.

This prayer is sung during the birthday celebrations
of the prophet Muhammad. It can also be associated
with celebrations at the time of the festival of
Eid-ul-Fitr. Sing it unaccompanied and aim for a
regular beat and clear singing.

A happy Eid   Khusir Idd

Music and words by Kazi Nazrul, arranged by Jean Gilbert,
translated from Bengali by Hiron Alam

Joyfully

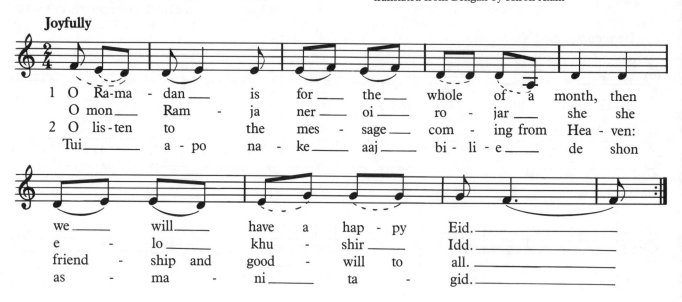

1 O Ra-ma - dan___ is for___ the___ whole of a month, then
  O mon___ Ram - ja ner___ oi___ ro - jar___ she she
2 O lis-ten to the mes - sage___ com - ing from Hea - ven:
  Tui___ a - po na - ke___ aaj___ bi - li - e___ de shon

we___ will___ have a hap - py Eid._____
e - lo___ khu - shir___ Idd._____
friend - ship and good - will to all._____
as - ma - ni___ ta - gid._____

Each verse is repeated and the first verse is sung
again at the end. Add any kind of percussion that
will add gaiety to this lovely Eid song.
e.g.

tambourine

triangle or bells

shakers

Younger children can join in, keeping time by
patting their knees or clapping hands and tapping
knees alternatively.

Suggested accompaniment

chime bars or glockenspiel

A beautiful day   Khushir Din

Music and words by Hiron Alam

Gaily but not too fast

This is our ho-li-day, fes-ti-val Eid day, We can eat Kor-ma,
Ei - der — din — aj - ke — tai — Kor - ma — Pu - lau,

Pu - lau — Fir - ni, There is no end of hap - pi - ness.
Fir - ni khai — Khu - shir — shi - ma nai re — nai —

Where can we find such a beau - ti - ful day? Where can we find such a beau - ti - ful day?
a - mon — din ar — ko - thay — pai a - mon — din ar — ko - thay — pai.

This happy song refers to some of the traditional foods that can be eaten during the Eid festival (see *Festival food* page 162).

After the first prayers on the first morning of Eid-ul-Fitr everyone goes to visit families and friends who live nearby. Everyone visits and if families are not in because they are visiting too, then you just go on to the next house! Traditionally sweetmeats are offered during these morning visits. If there are visitors in the house just before the Eid meal, then, again traditionally, they are invited to stay to the meal.

Suggested accompaniment

xylophone

This accompaniment underlines the shape of the tune, which goes up in a repeating pattern from bottom C to top C (bar 8) and then descends quickly to bottom C with the same rhythmic pattern.

Add small hand percussion like bongo drums and finger cymbals to the basic beat:

165

The Eid moon   Eider Chand

Music and words by Hiron Alam.
English words and arrangement by Jean Gilbert

Happily

I can see the Eid moon shin-ing high,_____
Eid - er chand____ oi dak - ha jay oi je_____

Show me where it shines up in the sky._____
Kot - hay chand____ khu - sir chand____ koi - re_____

From to - day we will sing and play, we will all be friends to - geth - er.
Aj - ker di - ne____ band - hu mor - a____ ay re sha - kal bhai - re

I can see the Eid moon shin-ing high,_____
Eid - er chand____ oi dak - ha jay oi je_____

Show me where it shines up in the sky._____
Kot - hay chand____ khu - sir chand____ koi - re_____

The new moon marks the end of Ramadan when Muslims begin to prepare for the festival of Eid-ul-Fitr.

The beginning and ending of this song is in the form of a conversation between two people. The children could be divided into two groups for these parts and join together to sing the middle line.

Suggested percussion

finger cymbals or bells throughout except *line 3*

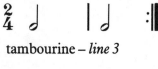

tambourine – *line 3*

Recorder

This tune could be played by an older child on the recorder.

Eid dance

Join hands in a circle.

Line 1   Seven steps to the left and stop
Line 2   Seven steps to the right and stop
Lines 3, 4   (repeat) Clap hands and skip into the centre and out, then skip round with a partner
Line 5   Seven steps to the left and stop
Line 6   Seven steps to the right and stop

Background information

The festival of Carnival is celebrated in many
countries where the dominant faith is Roman
Catholicism. The biggest and most elaborate of all
the Carnivals is the one that is held every year in
Trinidad. This great popular event attracts
thousands of people who come from all parts of the
Caribbean and further afield to watch the parades of
the masqueraders, to listen to the steelbands and
calypso singers and to participate in the street
marching, singing, dancing and evening revelry.

Carnival, meaning 'farewell to the flesh' (from
the Latin *carne vale*), was adopted by the Roman
Catholic Church as a pre-Lenten festival when
religious sanction was given to the pagan custom of
'Saturnalia' now thought to be the origin of this
festival. Christian converts were allowed two days
of feasting and merrymaking before the forty days
of fasting and repentance of Lent.

Evidence of Carnival celebrations in Trinidad
dates back to 1783 when French speaking
immigrants arrived on the island. This was the time
of the development of the sugar plantations for
which thousands of West Africans were captured by
the white settlers and forced into slavery. Their
participation in the festival brought a strong African
element to the rhythm of the music and dances and
the influence of the Afro-Caribbean people began to
show in their adaptation of European costumes for
the festival masquerade after emancipation in 1834.
The abolition of slavery created a new class of
freemen; it also created a work force vacuum which
was filled by new immigrants from China, Portugal,
Madeira, India and by free negroes from the U.S.A.

and Africa. Thus the present participants in the
Trinidad Carnival add a richness to the music and
masquerading that makes it one of the greatest
annual theatrical events of all time.

Today there are three main days of carnival
celebrations which follow many days of pre-carnival
events that are integral to the festival:

Carnival Sunday
Dimanche Gras. People arrive in Port of Spain, the
capital, and in all the other major towns. The day is
given over to meeting friends and going to dances
and parties.

Carnival Monday
Jour Ouvert (J'Ouvert – locally). This is the
opening of Carnival, the official beginning of the
'street festival'. The morning begins with street
dancing called 'jump up' to the music of the
steelbands. The afternoons are spent relaxing and
getting ready for evening activities, often more
'jumping'. (Each town has special traffic
regulations.)

Carnival Tuesday
Mardi Gras. This is the climax of the festival when
the masqueraders parade their exotic costumes
through the streets to end up in a large local park,
Queen's Park Savannah in the capital, where the
judging of the contestants in the numerous
competitions is held.

There is a special children's carnival held the
previous Saturday when prizes are given for the best
costumed child. This is also the climax of three to
six weeks pre-Carnival events.

Although Carnival is celebrated in February in
Trinidad, the summer term might be a more

suitable time to introduce it into the school, especially if an out-of-doors masquerade is a popular idea; a warm dry day, preferably with a bit of sunshine, would certainly help to create a carnival atmosphere for the children. Carnival is celebrated in London on August Bank Holiday and so to children in this country this is the time of year that is associated with this festival. Whenever you decide to introduce Carnival you could:

1 Run a competition for the best or most interestingly dressed boy or girl. As in Trinidad, these could be the Carnival King and Queen. In fairness to each child it might be necessary to produce the costumes at school or to stipulate how much parental help there should be.
2 Give a prize to or commend the child who has made the best 'old mas' costume from odds and ends brought from home; this might be the funniest one or the one that best disguises the wearer. This idea reflects the old masqueraders' custom of visiting private homes after dinner in disguise and seeing who could remain incognito the longest. Nowadays these costumes have become part of the main street masquerades.
3 Choose a Calypso King and Queen – the child who writes a good carnival poem or who creates some good sounds to accompany a poem.

Younger children will all want to become Kings and Queens. Each school will decide what kind of Kings and Queens they will have and how many; perhaps every child should have a chance to become one.

Art and craft

Make a frieze of all the children in the kind of costumes they hope to wear at the school carnival, build it up from their own large paintings or collage work.

Older children would also be interested in the various characters that, over the years, have become a traditional part of the Trinidad Masquerade. The outfits are an outlet for satire and buffoonery and masqueraders will take on the character of the costume they wear and practise for days before.

They may sometimes parade the same costume each year and eventually become known as that particular character.

Pierrot Granade   *Jab Molassi*   *Midnight Robber*

Pierrot Grenade
Pierrot Grenade is a boastful scholar. He parodies Pierrot his elegant brother and the inhabitants of Grenada, a neighbouring island. He can also be a comic poet; his dress is usually baggy, covered in strips of cloth and sometimes hung with tins and small boxes. He wears an old felt or straw hat and a grotesque face mask. He is very vain despite his untidy appearance.

Jab Molassi
Jab Molassi derives from the term 'Molasses Devil', so called because of the sticky black substance daubed over the player's body. It is thought that the use of soot and molasses to blacken the body might be one of the freedom symbols used in the masquerade; the cultivation of sugar cane from which molasses is produced was the job of the plantation slaves. The chains clearly relate to slavery. On Carnival days this character prances through the streets threatening to smear his grease over the clothes of the onlookers who do not hand over some of their cash. He has a long stiff tail, carries a trident and dances with strong rhythmic pelvic movements.

Midnight Robber

The dress of this character evolved from the simple cowboy outfit. It now consists of an Elizabethan doublet and breeches, a large elaborate hat and shoes that look like an animal with roving eyes. A flowing cape, revolver, wooden money box in the shape of a coffin and a whistle (blown constantly) completes the outfit. The Robber is a talkative, bragging character who tries to extort as much money as he can from people he accosts with the weapon he carries – often a dagger.

Other traditional carnival characters are *Minstrels, Bat, Dragon, Wild Indian, King Sailor, Flag Woman*. The latter dresses exotically in a tight fitting costume and leads the steelband.

With younger children it is probably best to stick to characters that they know and for which costumes or token costumes are easy.

Language

The language of the West Indies is called *creole* (meaning locally born), patois or dialect. Each island has its own language which has evolved as a result of the many different nationalities living there. Thus the creole is conditioned by whichever language is used locally, English, French, Spanish, Dutch, etc. It is often referred to as 'pidgin' or 'broken' English because much of the vocabulary is common to both languages, but it conforms to its own rules of grammar and cannot be compared to standard English.

The steel band

Steelband music comes from the Caribbean, from the island of Trinidad. It is an exciting and original type of folk music and although the bands that we hear in Britain are a relatively recent phenomenon, they have been an important part of the music of Trinidad since the Second World War.

Music had always been important in the lives of Africans and naturally flourished when freedom was granted to the slaves in Trinidad in 1833. They made music with the bamboo that was readily available, cutting and tuning the poles and forming **Tamboo Bamboo** bands. When these were banned by the government on the grounds that the excitement they caused might lead to riots, the islanders sought other ways of making music, trying anything that would produce an acceptable sound – bottles, tins, even dustbins and rubbish bins. It is probable that these experiments alerted them to the potential of the oil drum, for it was during and after the Second World War that these empty drums, abandoned as rubbish by the Americans who had been based on the island, were found to be ideal for making instruments. Whatever the circumstances or coincidences, the steel band came into being and was officially recognized in 1962 by the first government after the granting of independence.

There are now many steel bands all over the world playing anything from calypso to classical and pop, and every two years a steelband festival of a very high standard is held in the republic of Trinidad and Tobago. They are one of the highlights of Carnival and at this time of year a regular band of fifty players may grow to two hundred or over. They have an important part to play in the devising of a number of 'road marches' for the procession, and much practice and planning goes into preparations to accompany the thousands of masqueraders.

Steelbanders call their music **Pan**; this is what an oil drum is called when it has been prepared for playing. Making a pan is very hard work. First of all the top is 'sunk' or beaten into its correct shape with a sledge-hammer, then the position of the notes marked. A steel punch and hammer are used to shape these sections. The pan is then burnt and cooled off with water to give a better tone when it is later tuned. It is cut to the right length – larger pans give the lower notes – and finally tuned with a small hammer, a long and careful process to produce fine-sounding pans. There are several different kinds of pan that make up the main sections of a steelband, each designed to play at certain pitches. (*The Steel Band* by John Bartholomew published by O.U.P. has a simple description of this process and plenty of background information on the steel band).

Steel bands have been playing in Britain since the early 1950s and they are playing an increasingly important part in the musical life of many of our schools. Many authorities like the Inner London Education Authority have been especially supportive and the Commonwealth Institute organizes festivals for both school and adult bands.

Festival food

Coconuts are a local product in the West Indies and are the basic ingredient of many national dishes. Try to use freshly grated coconut for these two recipes. Saw the coconut carefully in half, remove the inside for cooking and smooth down the outside coating of the two half shells. You now have another percussion instrument to use with your songs and singing games.

Coconut biscuits

100g (4 oz) self raising flour
50g (2 oz) margarine
50g (2 oz) coconut
40g (just under 2 oz) sugar
2 tablespoons milk

METHOD
1 Sift the flour into a bowl and rub in the margarine.
2 Add the sugar and coconut and mix well.
3 Add enough milk to bind into a firm mixture.
4 Knead on a floured board until smooth.
5 Roll out to 1 cm thickness and make individual biscuits with pastry cutters.
6 Place on a greased baking tray and bake for 15 minutes in a moderately hot oven 340°F, gas mark 4. Makes about 24 biscuits.

Sugar cakes

200g (8 oz) grated coconut
300g (12 oz) granulated sugar
150ml milk (a good ½ cup: slightly less with fresh coconut)
pinch ground ginger
food dye (optional)

METHOD
1 Bring the sugar and milk to boil in a saucepan, stirring slowly until the sugar is completely dissolved and the mixture begins to thicken a little.
2 Remove from heat and add the coconut, ginger and (optional) food dye. Stir thoroughly until well blended.
3 Drop teaspoonfuls on to a greased tin and leave to set. Remove with a wooden spatula. Makes about 36 small cakes.

Other Carnival dishes

Fish from the Caribbean and Atlantic abound all the year round and feature in all Caribbean cooking. Salt fish, used originally as the main protein food for slaves and domestic servants, is popular today and is the basis for small seasoned fish balls served as cocktail snacks. Soak the fish well, mix with flour, beaten egg and milk, drop teaspoonfuls into hot fat and fry on both sides until golden brown. Stick cocktail sticks into the fish balls and eat while still warm or serve cold later.

A traditional meal at Carnival is 'cook-up' or Pelau which is rice, pigeon peas and meat prepared like the Spanish paella from which it is derived. Parents or local people with the 'know how' could be invited to prepare a meal working with the children in very small groups in school.

Me stone is me stone

Singing game from Trinidad

Me[1] stone is me stone Miss Ma - ry, Me stone is me stone Miss Ma - ry,

Me stone is me stone Miss Ma - ry, Pass um[2] dung[3] is me stone Miss Ma - ry.

1 me = my
2 um = them
3 dung = down

This song is one of a number used for stone-passing games, or 'pound-stone games' as they are called in Trinidad. They are popular among children and young adults of all ages.

The children sit in a circle, each one holding a large stone, or something similar. They all sing in strict rhythm. When the rhythm is established the game begins. Each child slaps his 'stone' down in front of the child sitting *to his right* and picks up the 'stone' placed in front of him by the child *on his left*. This continues to the rhythm of the singing until the signal to stop, when each player slaps the 'stone' down in front of himself.

Variations include passing the 'stones' to the left and increasing or slowing down the tempo.

The rhythm for the stone-passing could be underlined by a drum or tambour:

A leader could be chosen to stop and start the game using the rhythm of the song to say:
  'Get ready to start – GO'
  'Get ready to stop – STOP'

Johnny Grotto

Traditional, arranged by Gareth Walters

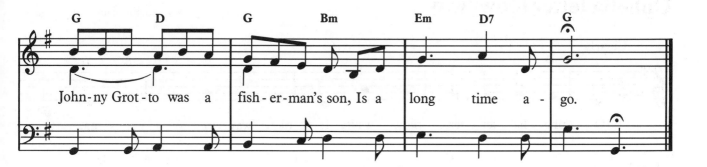

Johnny Grotto was a fisherman's son, Is a long time ago.

2 De sea is so rough an me han is so tough,
 Yea, yea, yea meh boy,
 De sea is so rough an me han is so tough,
 Is a long time ago.

3 We catch plenty fish, we go cook a nice dish,
 Yea, yea, yea meh boy,
 We catch plenty fish, we go cook a nice dish,
 Is a long time ago.

4 De lan is in sight, we go reach before night.
 Yea, yea, yea meh boy,
 De lan is in sight, we go reach before night,
 Is a long time ago.

This shanty from Tobago, Trinidad's sister island, underlines the importance of fishing to an island community. Groups of fishermen sing it to help them pull in the nets. Let the children do the actions while they sing; you could also use the song for rowing, throwing out the nets and sorting the fish.

Let individual children have a turn at singing some of the solo parts if they are ready to sing on their own, or choose groups of children for the verses.

Suggested percussion

tambourine   guiro

Tuned percussion

The following pattern played on a xylophone, glockenspiel or chime bars will fit the simple harmony of this work song:

Ophelia letter blow 'way

Singing game from Trinidad

1 O - phe - lia' let - ter blow 'way[1], It blow 'way in A - ri - ma, O - phe - lia let - ter blow 'way, It blow 'way in A - ri - ma, It blow 'way in A - ri - ma, It blow 'way in A - ri - ma.

2 Ophelia whe'[2] you'[3] letter?
It blow 'way in Arima,
Ophelia whe' you' letter?
It blow 'way in Arima,
It blow 'way in Arima,
It blow 'way in Arima.

1 'way = away
2 whe' = where's
3 you' = your

The central theme of this game – the search for something 'lost' – is common to several Trinidad dead-wake singing games. The 'letter blow 'way' is a poetical description of death, and the games are really simulated searches to find the dead relative.

The children sit in a fairly close circle. A small object – the 'letter' – is shown to one of the children chosen to be Ophelia, who then goes away while the letter is hidden in a conspicuous place such as someone's head or lap. The singing begins as Ophelia returns to the circle to start the search; it gets very quiet as the player moves close to the 'letter' and louder as he moves away. The next Ophelia is the one on whom the 'letter' is discovered. The children might like to use their own names for this game.

Ibo bo lay lay

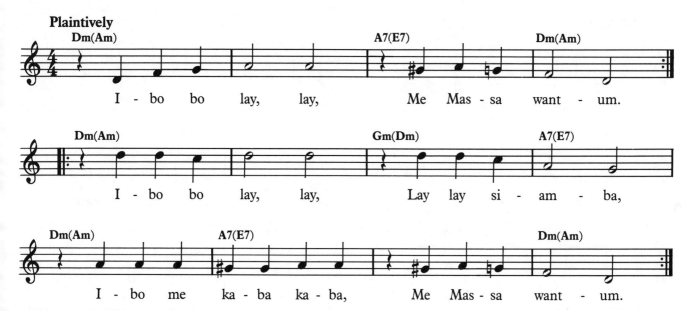

This plaintive, haunting tune is thought to have originated from the Ibo tribe in Nigeria from where many Africans were enslaved and imported to Trinidad in the 18th century. It can still be heard in many rural parts of Trinidad. The actual meaning of the words used has long since been forgotten.

When the children know the tune well, divide them into two groups so that each repeat phrase can be sung as an echo. Keep the rhythm stable with a slow drum beat played on the first beat of every bar.

Younger children may prefer to sing in the lower key of Am (chords in brackets).

Recorders

Older recorder players will enjoy the tune once they have mastered the G♯.

Little Sandy girl

Singing game from Tobago

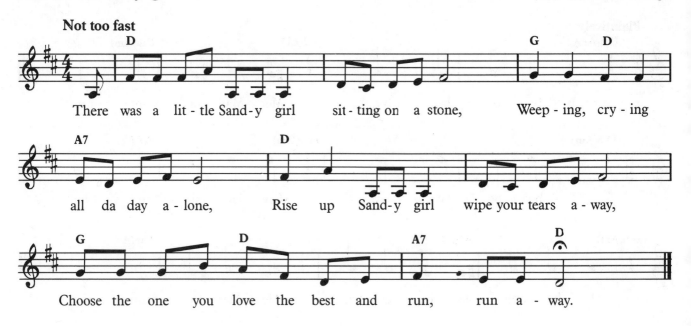

Not too fast

There was a lit-tle Sand-y girl sit-ting on a stone, Weep-ing, cry-ing all da day a-lone, Rise up Sand-y girl wipe your tears a-way, Choose the one you love the best and run, run a-way.

This singing game was collected from a play group at Charlotteville, Tobago. It is thought to be related to 'Little Sally Waters', a British traditional singing game and is one of many variants on this theme.

The children choose a 'Sandy girl' to sit on a 'stone' in the middle of their circle. She pretends to cry while the other children sing and walk round in the circle. At 'Rise up . . .' Sandy girl stands up, dries her eyes and chooses one of the children in the circle to run away with. That child then becomes the next 'Sandy girl' as the game begins again.

Linky Loo

Unaccompanied

All a-long, all a-long, all a-long all a-long, all a-long, all a-long Lin-ky Loo.

Lin - ky Loo how ma-ny have you? Lin - ky Loo how ma-ny have you? I'll

bet a - ny man a pint of beer, there are no more than thir - ty-two.

This game is played with pencil and paper by any number of players who sit around in a circle and sing while making strokes on the paper. At the end of the song, players count strokes which should number 32. Those who fail to reach this number are out. Players sing faster as the game continues. The one who gets 32 strokes the greatest number of times is the winner.

You could alter the number – and change the name if necessary – to suit the abilities of your group of children.

Congo Tay

Single player	One day, one day.
Players	Congo Tay.
Single player	I went to the bay.
Players	Congo Tay.
Single player	I saw Miss Lucy.
Players	Congo Tay.
Single player	With a brood of chickens.
Players	Congo Tay.
Single player	I ask her for one, She won't give me one.
Players	Congo Tay.
Single player	And I'll take, I'll take.

Players stand in single file behind their leader, each holding the waist of the player in front. The single player stands facing the line.

As the single player begins to chant her line, the leader stretches her arms crosswise in protection of her brood and they all begin to sway from side to side. When the single player says she'll take, the brood scatter and she tries to catch one. The one caught helps her to catch other players and the game continues until all the players have been caught and the leader alone remains. She then becomes the single player and the game starts all over again.

Sly Mongoose

Jamaican folk song in calypso style

Sly Mon - goose, ___ your name gone a - broad,

Sly Mon - goose ___ your name gone a - broad.

Mon - goose slip in - to Bed - ward kit - chen, Steal out one of his right - eous chick - en,

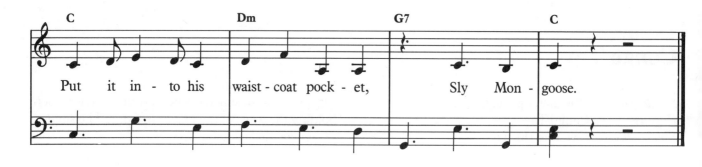

Put it in - to his waist - coat pock - et, Sly Mon - goose.

The melody of this traditional Jamaican song is in the calypso style. The mongoose referred to is a government official who tried to seduce one of the prophet Bedward's daughters. The song has been chosen as one that would provide a simple enough outline for teachers to encourage their children to make up their own calypso.

e.g. Orange class from Canonbury school,
Orange class from Canonbury school,
We went in the coach to the seaside,
We went for a swim, it was high tide,
We played all the day at the seaside,
Orange class.

The complete song can be found in *Mango Spice* (A. & C. Black), which also contains another suitable tune for older children, 'Dip an' fall back'.

Suggested percussion

maracas

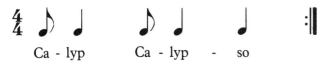

claves/tambourine

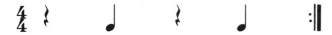

Calypso

The Calypso is unique to Trinidad where it has been sung for over 180 years, though it has now spread to many other islands and has been influenced by other styles such as, for instance, soca, which is a combination of soul and calypso. Its roots, like those of the blues and mento, are a style of dance and song indigenous to Jamaica. They can be traced to the folk songs and folk music of the Afro-West Indian slaves, with their bouncy rhythms and their A–B call-and-response work patterns.

In these songs it is the words that are important; the melody, often one that has been used time and time again, merely provides a framework on which the singer, a calypsonian, can weave his story. The songs consist of a number of verses followed by a set refrain. The verses can be humorous, complaining or constitute a protest or satirical comment on any event, be it political, sporting or domestic. The calypsonian can take any subject he pleases but he must also be a virtuoso in the art of instant composition. Traditionally the words are not written down and the singer can run the risk of drying up or 'busting'.

Calypso plays an important part in the Trinidad Carnival. There are special calypso centres, called **tents**, and on the Sunday before Carnival there is a gala performance featuring the seven best calypsonians who compete for the title of Calypso King or Queen. There is also the people's choice of the best calypso. This singer then becomes the 'Roadmarch King' and his calypso is played, sung and danced to during the street parade.

More Caribbean songs

Each book in this series contains 12 Jamaican folk songs with melody line, guitar chords and suggestions for percussion. They include:

Jane and Louisa
Brown gal in de ring
Linstead Market
Banyan tree
Day oh

The songs outlined in this section are from the islands of Trinidad and Tobago. The following notes include references to material from other areas of the Caribbean to widen the choice of further songs.

Mango Spice
(A. & C. Black)

An invaluable collection containing 44 well arranged songs and an informative introduction to the music, style and background of Caribbean singing. It includes the following favourites:

Day oh, day oh
Tinga layo
Hill an gully rida
There's a brown girl in the ring
Oh freedom

There is also a section of Anancy stories, each with an accompanying song. This collection serves a wide age range.

Rain falling, sun shining
by Odette Thomas (Bogle-L'Ouverture Publications Ltd)

This book contains song-rhymes representative of Caribbean folk culture and chosen to appeal to people of all ages, especially the 4 to 11-year-olds.

Buddy Lindo
by John Harvey (O.U.P.)

16 folk songs of Trinidad and Tobago suitable for infants and lower juniors. Clear melody line with guitar chords. Includes 'Gipsy in de moonlight'.

Brown gal in de ring
Alle, alle, alle
Beeny Bud
Dandy Shandy
collected and arranged by Olive Lewin (O.U.P.)

Poems

Boat-builder

Boat-builder,
Boat-builder,
Build me a boat
As you rap
And you tap
And you hum.

Boat-builder,
Boat-builder,
Build me a boat
And I'll pay you a very large sum.

Please make it a sloop
With a mat and a sail
And a small jib at the bow.
On the stern, put a rudder,
A stick I can move
To steer her anyhow.

Boat-builder,
Boat-builder,
Build me a boat
As you rap
And you tap
And you hum.

Boat-builder,
Boat-builder,
Build me a boat
And I'll pay you a very large sum.

This poem was written by a student-teacher for
primary children in the Caribbean; its purpose was
to help them learn the parts of a sloop and it also
provided the basis for a skipping game. It invites
any form of circle game with a boat-builder in the
middle doing the actions.

Carnival in Trinidad

Romance in the tropic air
Here and there and everywhere
Everyone is on the go,
Pans to tune, costumes to sew;
Money lending
Wire bending
Metal sheeting
In the beating
Bleachers building,
Coaches gilding.
Miles of gold and silver braid
Heralding the masquerade.

Sensuous calypso beat
Echoing through every street,
Youth and age alike will be
Gyrating round in ecstasy
Steelbands clashing
Jab-jabs lashing
Robbers cracking
Coons click-clacking
Witches croaking
Jester joking
Imps and devils on parade
All part of the masquerade.

Ancient monarchs, ladies fair,
Dragons belching red hot air,
Grotesque mok-jumbies tall
Red Indians, wigwams and all
Groggy fellow
Strumming 'cello
Police chasing
Children racing
Parents hissing.
Lovers kissing
Devotee and renegade –
All part of the masquerade.

Share our nation's festival,
Heritage of great and small,
Most exciting of them all:
Blaze of glory – Carnival.

Older children will enjoy the Carnival 'feel' that
this poem conjures up. Read a selection to younger
children – the first and last verses for example.
   Encourage the children to write about their own
carnival and shape into a class poem.

181

Listen

Shhhhhhhh!
Sit still, very still
And listen.
Listen to wings
Lighter than eyelashes
Stroking the air.
Know what the thin breeze
Whispers on high
To the coconut trees.
Listen and hear.

This poem highlights quiet sounds and presents the teacher with a golden opportunity to focus on these delicate 'thin' sounds that will contrast with the rowdiness evoked by the Carnival poem. Listen to quiet sounds around your own school. Make quiet sounds with voices and instruments. Ask the children to find out how many different quiet sounds they can get from any one instrument. Then select with them suitable sounds to build into a quiet sound picture, for example:

Up in the trees	Suggested sounds
wind	voices *shhhh, oooo, nnnn, mmmm*
insects	voices *ssss, mmmm, nnnn* or quiet shakers/sand block/drum head scratched or stroked
birds' wings	brush stroking a cymbal, rubbing hands
bird song	gentle recorder trill or sounds from a small glockenspiel or bells
leaves	shakers, voices, sand block or crumpling tissue paper

Divide the children into small groups. Encourage the children to listen all the time as they contribute freely in each group – the sounds come and go giving the effect of a continually changing pattern of very quiet, controlled sounds.

Evening sounds
heard from a block of flats in a big city

	Suggested sounds
traffic	voices *mmmm, tttt, ssss, hhhh*
police car (in the distance)	chimes or glockenspiel played with a soft beater – notes A C or G E

people going home	very quiet clappers played at different speeds
people talking	muted voices talking/whispering
birds roosting	voices *ssss, tttt, ks ks ks ks* or chimes/triangles played with the sound deadened by a held hand

any other sounds relevant to your neighbourhood

Again divide into small groups. In this case the traffic could rumble in the background all the time while the other sounds come and go. These quiet sounds demand a great deal of concentration from the children and they must resist the temptation to get louder when contributing in a group. Make sure, therefore, that you hear all the groups and recognize each child's contribution.

Iguana!
Iguana!
prehistoric memory!
light green,
dark green,
shadow of earth's history!
no more a monster –
though spine's frills often fright!
but plants
and leaves –
and fruit-eater;
tree dweller –
out of sight!

I spy
a humming bird,
he seems to hang before a flower,
you'd think it was a trick!
but no! his wings –
they move so fast –
they hold him in the air
while with his long beak,
slightly curved,
he sucks the nectar
there!

These interesting and instructional verses are selected from others in a beautifully illustrated book for primary children dealing with the flora and fauna common to the West Indies.

RESOURCES

Introduction

This resource list has been compiled to give some idea of the range of books and materials currently available, and of other types of assistance that might be helpful in preparing schemes of work around each festival. It is not a fully comprehensive coverage; in any case changes are continually taking place.

In addition to the specialist sources and organizations named, various other types of assistance might be available locally. It is impossible to list these in detail, but they could include:

— Local Education Authority advisers and inspectors
— Local public libraries, who should be able to obtain any of the books quoted in the list, even if not in their stocks. Some libraries hold collections of records and cassettes
— Teachers' resource centres and education libraries
— Local ethnic groups and specialist shops
— Parents are usually delighted to be involved. They might be willing to lend books, records, costumes and other items of significance to a particular festival

Each festival is covered by a separate section. Where sources relate to more than one festival they are listed in the General section.

General

For teachers

Festivals and Customs
  Norman J. Bull (R.M.E.P.)
The Living Festivals
  Teachers Books cover Hindu, Christian and Jewish festivals. Jon Mayled (R.M.E.P.)
SHAP Calendar of Religious Festivals
  Clive A. Lawton (Commission for Racial Equality)
Exploring Red Letter Days
  D. Taylor (Lutterworth Educational)
Faiths and Festivals
  Martin Palmer (Ward Lock Educational)
Festivals and Celebrations
  Rowland Purton (Blackwell)
The Dictionary of Beliefs
  Richard Kennedy (Ward Lock Educational)
Exploring Religion
  A series of books for use with older children. Includes Festivals, Worship, People, Signs and Symbols. Olivia Bennett (Bell & Hyman)
Six Religions in the Twentieth Century
  W. Owen Cole (Hulton Eductional)
Light the Candles
  Songs of Praise and Ceremony from around the World. June B. Tillman (Cambridge University Press)
A Musical Calendar of Festivals
  Barbara Cass-Beggs (Ward Lock Educational)

MAAS Register
Presents a comprehensive list of names and addresses in the field of Minority Arts: dance, education, media, music, print and the visual arts. Produced as a result of a report commissioned by the Commission for Racial Equality. (Minorities Arts Advisory Service, 28 Shacklewell Lane, London E8 2EZ)

For children

Festivals – My First Library
(Macdonald Educational)
Feasting and Fasting – 'Religious Topic' series
Jon Mayled (Wayland)
This series also includes books on religious dress, festivals, food and beliefs.
Strands
Series introducing people from different cultural backgrounds living in Britain. Each book features the everyday life of a family. (A. & C. Black)

Miscellaneous

A.I.M.E.R. (Access to Information on Multi-cultural Education Resources)
This project helps teachers to find out about and share resources appropriate to multi-cultural education.
The postal enquiry service offers teachers a print-out based on their requirements.
Sue Williams, A.I.M.E.R. Faculty of Education & Community Studies, The University of Reading, Bulmershe Court, Earley, Reading, RG6 1HY
Festivals Around the World
Pack 6. International Picture Charts (Macmillan Educational)
Pictorial charts and information leaflets from Pictorial Charts Educational Trust, 27 Kirchen Road, London W13. Packs are available on Jewish, Islamic, Hindu, Christian, Chinese festivals.
Many public libraries are now providing services in terms of books, newspapers, periodicals and sound recordings for ethnic minorities. Some of the children's libraries offering this service have links with the local teachers' resource centres.

Harvest Festival

For teachers

The Grains are Great Foods
A booklet on cereal crops – wheat, rice, maize, oats. Kelloggs Company, Public Relations Dept., Stretford, Manchester M32 8RA
Farms and Schools
This educational charity provides a number of cheap booklets on different aspects of agriculture at different levels. Send s.a.e. to The Association of Agriculture, 16/20 Strutton Ground, London, SW1P 2HP.
Fun with Seeds
Leisure Craft series 47 (Search Press)

For children

Harvest festival
From the 'Celebrations' series. Lynne Hannington and Renu Nagrath (A. & C. Black)
Harvest
From the 'Celebrations' series. Hilary Lee-Corbin (Wayland)
Autumn
Althea (Souvenir Press)
In the Autumn
Peggy Blakely (A. & C. Black)

Recorded music

The Four Seasons   Vivaldi
The Seasons   Glazunov
The Seasons — Autumn Song   Tchaikovsky
Symphony No. 6 (The Pastoral) — Third movement ('Peasants' merrymaking')   Beethoven

Jewish Festivals

For teachers

Succot: Chanukah: Passover
From the 'Living Festivals' series. Lynne Scholefield (R.M.E.P.)
Jewish Lives
From the 'Living the Faith' series. John Coutts (Oliver & Boyd)
Jewish Festivals
From the 'Festivals' series. R. Turner (Wayland)

Judaism
    From the 'Religions of the World' series. M. Domnitz (Wayland)
Jewish Living
    Reuben Turner (J.N.F. Publishing Company)

For children

Sam's Passover
    From the 'Celebrations' series. Lynne Hannigan (A. & C. Black)
Matza and Bitter Herbs
    From the 'The Way We Live' series. Lawton/Cormack (Hamish Hamilton)
I am a Jew
    From the 'My Belief' series. Clive Lawton (Franklin Watts)

Recorded music and A.V. material

Jewish Song Calendar
    Cassette accompanying a book of selected festival songs. (J.N.F. Publishing Company)
Especially Wonderful Days
    Cassette of festival songs with song book for primary grades. (Jewish Educational Bureau)
Living Judaism
    Tape/slide programme (23 mins). Description and explanation of the Jewish year with the festivals. (The Council of Christians and Jews, 1, Dennington Park Road, London NW6)
Judaism — A Way of Life
    Colour filmstrip with notes about the Jewish religion, its beliefs and ceremonies. (J.N.F. Publishing Company)
Chag Lataf — Holiday Songs   CBS 53825
    30 songs sung in Hebrew including several featured in the Jewish sections of this book. Available from some specialist shops supplied by Jerusalem The Golden. See *Useful addresses*.

Useful addresses

Central Jewish Lecture & Information Committee, Woburn House, Upper Woburn Place, London WC1 (tel: 01–387 3952)
Pamphlets, booklets and filmstrips on Judaism.

Jewish Programme Materials Project (J.P.M.P.) 741 High Road, London N12 (tel: 01–446 1477)
Books, pamphlets, leaflets, filmstrips, slides, audio-visual programmes on Judaism, Israel and Jewish history.

Jewish Educational Bureau, 8 Westcombe Avenue, Leeds LS8 2BS (tel: 0532 663613)
Books, filmstrips, cassettes and posters.

J.N.F. Publishing Company, Harold Poster House, Kingsbury Circle, London NW9 9SP (tel: 01–204 9911)
Books, pamphlets, posters, filmstrips and cassettes.

Israel Embassy, Information Department, 2 Palace Green, London W8 (tel: 01–937 8050)

Jerusalem The Golden, 146b Golders Green Road, London NW11 8HE (tel: 01–455 4960)
Books, crafts, records and cassettes on tourist, cantorial, Yiddish and children's music.

Hallowe'en

For teachers

Hallowe'en
    From the 'Festivals' series. Robin May (Wayland)
Hallowe'en, All Souls' and All Saints'
    From the 'Living Festivals' series. Antony Ewens (R.M.E.P.)

For children

Hallowe'en
    From the 'Celebrations' series. Hilary Lee-Corbin (Wayland)
The Return of the Witch
    Margaret Stuart Barry (Collins)
The Worst Witch   The Worst Witch Strikes Again
    Jill Murphy (Allison & Busby)
The Witch's Lost Spell Book
    Joan Cass (Hodder & Stoughton)
Meg and Mog books
    (Heinemann)

Recorded music

The Sorcerer's Apprentice   Dukas
Night on the Bare Mountain   Mussorgsky
Hansel and Gretel   Humperdinck
    For suggested excerpts see *Hansel and Gretel* notes, pages 46, 47.
Peer Gynt Suite — In the Hall of the Mountain King   Grieg
Danse Macabre   Saint-Saëns
Listen, Move and Dance (no. 4)   HMV CLP 3531
    Includes a series of electronic sound pictures that would provide several suitable themes for movement such as *A Magic Journey, Witches, Wizards, Alchemists* and *Sorcerers*.

Out of this World BBC REC 225
  This record includes a number of atmospheric sounds and effects useful for dramatic work with older children.

Diwali and Holi

For teachers

Hindu Festivals
  From the 'Festivals' series. S. Mitter (Wayland)
Indian Dance
  Two sets of charts associated with the stories of Diwali and Holi. Pictorial Charts Educational Trust, 27 Kirchen Road, London W13 0UD
The Ramayana
  For the teacher who is interested in reading the story in greater depth, this account provides a poetic prose reading of great beauty. Elizabeth Seeger (Dent)
Indian Music
  This short illustrated book from the series *Oxford Topics in Music* is both informative and practical. It is accompanied by a cassette containing recordings of the projects outlined in the book and examples of Indian music. Leela Floyd (O.U.P.)
Diwali; Holi
  From the 'Living Festivals' series (R.M.E.P.)
India — the Land and its People
  Natasha Talyarkhan (Macdonald Educational)

For children

The Ramayana
  Cartoon story from 'India' series. (R.M.E.P.)
Hanuman
  Anukshi Hora (B. R. Anada) available from Books from India Bookshop
Diwali
  From the 'Festival' series. Olivia Bennett (Macmillan Education)
Holi: Hindu Festival of Spring
  Bennett/Cormack (Hamish Hamilton)
The Lights of Diwali: The Holi Fire
  Two of the 'Citylinks' series. June Jones (Blackie)
India is My Country
  From the 'My Country' series. C. & B. Moon (Wayland)

I am a Hindu
  From the 'My Belief' series. Manju Aggarwal (Franklin Watts)

Recorded music

Raga Rang — A Tapestry of Indian Classical Instrumental Music
  EMI (India) ECSD 2773
Music from India EMI EASD 1356
  Ravi Shanka plays sitar accompanied by bass and tanpura. Any Ravi Shanka classical record is suitable.

Music for a Garba (pronounced Gerba), a Holi stick dance, can be found among recordings on the LP set Polydor 2675 213

There are two Diwali songs on the EMI record 33 ESX 14022
1. Ek Wott Bhi Diwali Thi
2. Mele Hain Chiraghonki

Useful addresses

The Commonwealth Institute, Kensington High Street, London W8 6NQ (tel: 01–603 4535)
Arranges visits to schools by Indian musicians and dancers.

The Institute of Indian Culture (Bharatiya Vidya Bhavan) 14a Castletown Road, London W14 (tel: 01–381 3086)

Government of India Tourist Office, 7 Cork Street, London W1 (tel: 01–437 3677)
Supplies brochures and information about India.

The Gramophone Company of India Limited, UK Branch, 1/3 Uxbridge Road, Hayes, Middlesex UB4 0SY (tel: 01–561 5922)
Supplies catalogues and further information.

Soma Books, 38 Kennington Lane, London SE11 4LS (tel: 01–735 2101)
Books and stories about India

Books from India Bookshop, 45 Museum Street, London WC1A 1LR (tel: 01–405 3784)

Christmas

For teachers

Christmas Customs Around the World
  Herbert H. Wernecke (Bailey Brothers & Swinfen)

Christmas
From the 'Living Festivals' series. Antony Ewens (R.M.E.P.)
Folk Costumes of the World
Robert Harrold/Phyllida Legg (Blandford Press)
Christmas and Festive Day Recipes
Sara Paston-Williams (David and Charles)

For children

The Christmas Book
Susan Baker (Macdonald Educational)
A Christmas Story
Brian Wildsmith (O.U.P.)
Christmas
From the 'Celebrations' series, Hilary Lee-Corbin (Wayland)
The Fir Tree
Hans Andersen (Kaye and Ward)
The Innkeeper's Daughter
Carol Greene (Concordia)
Lucy and Tom's Christmas
Shirley Hughes (Victor Gollancz)

Recorded music

Children's Corner — The Snow is Dancing (No. 4)   Debussy
Skaters' Waltz   Waldteufel
Lieutenant Kijé — Sleigh Ride   Prokofiev
The Seasons — Winter   Vivaldi
Sinfonia Antartica   Vaughan Williams
Short extracts to convey cold, ice, snow, winter bleakness
Les Patineurs   Meyerbeer
Fantasia on Christmas Carols   Vaughan Williams
Older children might enjoy some of this work, especially the final 'Wassail Song'.
Carol Symphony   Hely-Hutchinson
Carols are woven in and out of the music in each movement. If older children have learnt any of the carols they would enjoy short excerpts from a particular movement.

1st movement — *O, come all ye faithful*
2nd movement — *God rest ye merry, gentlemen*
3rd movement — *Noel, Noel*
4th movement — Excerpts from above

Amahl and the Night Visitors   Menotti
The theme of this children's opera is particularly relevant. The Three Kings visit Amahl, the small crippled son of a shepherdess, during their journey to the manger and rest at his home. Amahl decides to go with the Kings and offers his crutch as a gift for the baby king. He is overjoyed to discover that he has gained the use of his leg. Select short excerpts to illustrate the story.
Christmas Carol Records
There are many records available. Recordings of the choir of King's College, Cambridge or St Paul's Cathedral are beautiful. The Spinners have recorded a more homely offering — EMI SCX 6602.

Chinese New Year

For teachers

Chinese New Year
From the 'Living Festivals' series. Anne Bancroft (R.M.E.P.)
Buddhism
Trevor Ling (Ward Lock Educational)
Ancient China (Great Civilizations)
Robert Knox (Longman)
China in Pictures
Joanna Moore (Sterling Publishing)
We Live in China
Li Tsang (Wayland)

For children

A Family in China
From the 'Families Around the World' series. Jacobsen/Kristensen (Wayland)
China
From the 'Countries of the World' series. Julia Waterlow (Wayland)
Chinese New Year
From the 'Festival' series. Olivia Bennett (Macmillan Education)
The story about Ping
Marjorie Flack/Kurt Wiese (Puffin Books)
Little Chen and the Dragon Brothers
Adapted folk tale (Foreign Languages Press)
Ma Liang and his Magic Brush
Adapted folk tale (Foreign Languages Press)

Publications of Foreign Languages Press can be obtained through the Guanghwa Bookshop and the Society for Anglo-Chinese Understanding. See *Useful addresses*. There are many more very attractive picture story books available from these sources.

Recorded music

The Nutcracker Ballet Music — Chinese Dance   Tchaikovsky

Mother Goose Suite   Ravel
> The third section is based on the pentatonic five-note scale; the music describes a little Chinese Empress taking her bath to the sound of toy oriental music.

Chinese Classical Music   Lyrichord LLST 772
> Available through Collet's International Bookshop, Folk Music Department, 129/131, Charing Cross Road, London WC2H 0EQ

Chinese Classical Music   Fung Hang Records Ltd FHLP 222

Dragon Boat   Fung Hang Records Ltd PHLP 114
> The above two titles are selected from records and cassettes available from the Hong Kong Cultural Service. See *Useful addresses*.

Useful addresses

Hong Kong Cultural Service, 46 Gerrard Street, London W1 (tel: 01–734 5037)
Records, cassettes, books, cards, lanterns, miscellaneous items.

Guanghwa Company, Book and Record Shop, 7/9 Newport Place, London WC2 (tel: 01–437 3737)
Records, story books, cards, small lion heads and other miscellaneous items.

Society for Anglo-Chinese Understanding, 152 Camden High Street, London NW1
> (tel: 01–485 8236)
Books, cards, periodicals, miscellaneous items.

New Era Books, 203 Seven Sisters Road, London N4 (tel: 01–272 5894)

Hong Kong Government Office, 6 Grafton Street, London W1 (tel: 01–499 9821)

Raymond Man, 64 Neal Street, London WC2 (tel: 01–240 1776) Agent for Chinese musical intruments. Mr Man stocks an enormous range of authentic instruments from small bells to large drums. You can buy lion heads from him too.

Greek Festivals
> Part of the Cambridge Schools Classics Project. (Cambridge University Press)

For children

Greece is My Country
> From the 'My Country' series. B. & C. Moon (Wayland)

I am a Greek Orthodox
> Maria Roussou (Franklin Watts)

Rebecca is a Cypriot
> Nick McCarty (A. & C. Black)

The Biggest Bonfire in the World
> A story about Easter in Cyprus. Maria Roussou (Schools Council Publications Ltd)

Recorded music

Greek Popular and Folk Dances
> EMI 14C062–70007

Dances and Songs of the Cyprus Wedding
> Kerabnophone LPKC 1006
> Available from the Trehantiri Record Shop. See *Useful addresses*.

Children's Songs and Stories (in Greek)
> Refer to the Trehantiri Record Shop for these and other current records.

Useful addresses

Cyprus High Commission, 93 Park Street, London W1 (tel: 01–499 8272)

Greek Embassy, 1a Holland Park, London W11 (tel: 01–727 8040)

Greek Parents' Association, 22 Stuart Crescent, London N22 (tel: 01–889 1872)

Trehantiri Record Shop, 367 Green Lanes, London N4 (tel: 01–802 6530)

Zeno Bookshop, 6 Denmark Street, London WC2 (tel: 01–836 2522)

Easter in Cyprus

For teachers

The Orthodox Church
> Margaret Doak (R.M.E.P.)

Greece: The Land and its People
> One of the 'Countries' series. Jim Antoniou (Macdonald Educational)

Easter

For teachers

Easter
> From the 'Living Festivals' series. Norma Fairbairn and Jack Priestley (R.M.E.P.)

Easter
> From the 'Festivals' series. Julian Fox (Wayland)

For children

Projects for Easter
From the 'Seasonal Projects' series. Jean Cooke
(Wayland)
Easter
From the 'Celebrations' series. Hilary
Lee-Corbin (Wayland)
Easter
A story and activity book. Hobson/James
(Macdonald)
The Chicken and the Egg
One of the 'Nature's Way' series.
(Andre Deutsch)
Seeds and Seedlings
One unit from 'Teaching Primary Science'.
Dorothy Diamond (Macdonald Educational)
Plants and How they Grow
Series 651 'Natural History' (Ladybird)

Recorded music

Messiah   Handel
Very short excerpts e.g. the Halleluiah Chorus.
The Seasons — Spring   Vivaldi
Spring Song   Mendelssohn
Appalachian Spring   Copland
To the Spring (piano)   Grieg
Jesus Christ Superstar   Tim Rice and Andrew
Lloyd Webber
Catchy tunes e.g. 'What's the Buzz' and
'Hosanna'.
Godspell   Schwartz
Favourite tunes like 'Day by Day' and 'All Good
Gifts'.
Easter Parade   Irving Berlin
This song appears on many discs. Ask your
dealer what is currently available.

For movement

Snowflakes are falling   Debussy
Electronic rendering by Tomita.
The Hen   Respighi
Carnival of the Animals — Hens and Cocks
Saint-Saëns
Pictures at an Exhibition — Hatching Chicks
Mussorgsky

Eid-ul-Fitr

For teachers

The Muslim Guide
McDermott/Ahsan (The Islamic Foundation)
Islam for Children
Ahmad von Denffer (The Islamic Foundation)
Ramadan and Id-ul-Fitr
From the 'Living Festivals' series. Janis
Hannaford (R.M.E.P.)
Muslim Festivals
From the 'Festivals' series. M. Ahsan (Wayland)
A Muslim Family in Britain
Harrison/Shepherd (R.M.E.P.)

For children

Eid-ul-Fitr
From the 'Celebrations' series. Shusheila Stone
(A. & C. Black)
Ramadan and Eid-ul-Fitr
From the 'Festival' series. Olivia Bennett
(Macmillan Education)
I am a Muslim
From the 'My Belief' series. Manju Aggarwal
(Franklin Watts)

Recorded music

The following records contain Muslim songs in
Urdu:
Haj-e-Baitullah   EMI   S/MOCE 2017
Aaya Haj ka Maheena   EMI   EKDA 10016
Both the above are about the pilgrimage to Mecca
and are sung by Mohammed Rafi.
Ramzan Ka Haheena bara   EMI EKDA 10019
This record is about Ramadan.

For recorded Indian music see the Diwali section,
page 186.

Recordings of the Koran on both disc and cassette
are available from Muslim record shops and from
the Muslim Information Services. See *Useful
addresses*. If the children are going to listen to any
recording it is necessary for them to be as clean as
possible, at least to have washed their hands. Of
course the best arrangement is to invite a
representative from a local mosque to come into
school to talk to the children about the Koran and
to read excerpts from it to them.

Useful addresses

Muslim Information Services, 233 Seven Sisters Road, London N4 3RZ (tel: 01–263 3071)
Posters, Eid cards, colouring books, books in Arabic and English for adults and children.

Islamic Cultural Centre, Regents Lodge, 146 Park Road, London NW8 (tel: 01–724 3363)

Islamic Foundation, 223 London Road, Stoneygate, Leicester (tel: 0533 536354)

Pakistan Embassy, 35 Lowndes Square, London SW1 (tel: 01–235 2044)

Soma Books, 38 Kennington Lane, London SE11 (tel: 01–735 2101)

Bangladesh High Commission, 28 Queen's Gate, London SW7 (tel: 01–584 0081)

Indian Record House, 70 South Road, Southall, Middlesex UB1 1RD (tel: 01–571 1306)
Supplies catalogues of records, cassettes and books on Islam for use in schools.

Trinidad Carnival and Caribbean

For teachers

The Trinidad Carnival and Caribbean
Errol Hill (University of Texas Press, Austin and London)
The Caribbean
One of the 'Countries Special' series. Ken Campbell (Macdonald Educational)
The Caribbean People (Books 1 and 2)
Lennox Honychurch (Nelson)
Jamaican Music
One of the 'Oxford Topics in Music' series. Michael Burnett (O.U.P.)
Masquerade
Jeremy Taylor (Macmillan Caribbean)
The Steel Band
One of the 'Oxford Topics in Music' series. John Bartholomew (O.U.P.)
Steelbands and Reggae
One of the 'Longman Music Topics' series. Paul Farmer (Longman)
Caribbean Cookbook
Rita G. Springer (Pan Books)
Under the Mango Tree
Books 1 and 2: songs and poems. Mabel Segun and Neville Grant (Longman)

Once Below a Time
Telcine Turner (Macmillan Caribbean)
Listen to this Story
Tales from the West Indies. Grace Hallworth (Methuen)
Ears, Tails and Commonsense
Philip Sherlock (Deutsch)

For children

The Caribbean
John Griffiths (Wayland)
Trinidad and Tobago
Junior Social Studies Book 1 Palmer and Sieuchand (Collins Caribbean)
West Indies
Zaidee Lindsay (A. & C. Black)
Carnival
From the 'Festivals' series. Jon Mayled (Wayland)
Carnival
From the 'Festival' series. Olivia Bennett (Macmillan Education)
Caribbean Carnivals & Festivals
Macmillan Caribbean Colouring Book
Nini at Carnival
Errol Lloyd (Bodley Head)
The Carnival Kite
Grace Hallworth (Methuen)
Jafta Books
Hugh Lewin (Bell & Hyman)
Seven of us
One of the 'Strands' series. Story of a Jamaican family living in Britain. (A. & C. Black)

Recorded music

Brown Girl in the Ring, Rivers of Babylon K11120 WEA Records Ltd
Two sides of the popular Boney M recording.
Roots of Reggae Music from Jamaica Lyrichord LLST 7314
A Night in Jost Van Dyke Rounder 5002
Carnival in St Thomas.
Caribbean Folk Music (two sets) Ethnic Folkways Library FE 4533
Caribbean Songs and Games for Children Folkways Records FC 7856
Folkways records are not readily available in record shops in Britain but can be obtained through some specialist shops like the Folk Record Department of Collet's International Bookshop.

See *Specialist bookshops*. These and other suitable Folkways records might be obtained through local record libraries and resource centres.

Calypso records can be borrowed from the Commonwealth Institute. Because calypsos date very quickly there is a new turnover each year. Many people bring them back from Trinidad when they come. A classic, however, is *Mighty Sparrow: 25th Anniversary* (Kitt Records JAF001).

Useful addresses

The Commonwealth Institute, Kensington High Street, London W8 6NQ (tel: 01–603 4535) has a permanent exhibition which includes objects to touch, wear, play with, etc. There is a library and an education department which will arrange talks to schools or classes.

Trinidad and Tobago High Commission, 42 Belgrave Square, London SW1 (tel: 01–245 9351)

Commission for Racial Equality, Information Department, 10–12 Allington Street, London SW1E 5EH (tel: 01–828 7022)

Specialist bookshops

New Beacon Books, 76 Stroud Green Road, London N4 3EN (tel: 01–272 4889)

Walter Rodney Bookshop, 5a Chignall Place, London W13 0TJ (tel: 01–579 4920)

Headstart Books and Crafts, 25 West Green Road, London N15 (tel: 01–802 2838/9623)

Grass Roots Bookshop, 71 Golborne Road, London W10 (tel: 01–969 0687)

Sabarr Bookshop, 358 Coldharbour Lane, London SW9 (tel: 01–274 6785)

Collet's International Bookshop, 129/131 Charing Cross Road, London WC2 (tel: 01–734 0782/3)